HAL LEONARD
DULCIMER METHOD

SECOND EDITION

For Mountain Dulcimer

BY NEAL HELLMAN

ISBN 978-0-7935-3632-0

HAL•LEONARD®
CORPORATION
7777 W. BLUEMOUND RD. P.O. BOX 13819 MILWAUKEE, WI 53213

In Australia Contact:
Hal Leonard Australia Pty. Ltd.
4 Lentara Court
Cheltenham, Victoria, 3192 Australia
Email: ausadmin@halleonard.com.au

Visit Hal Leonard Online at
www.halleonard.com

ABOUT THE AUTHOR

Neal Hellman, nationally acclaimed performer and teacher of the mountain dulcimer, has been active in performing, writing, teaching, and recording acoustic music for the past 25 years throughout the United States, Europe, and New Zealand.

His recordings include *Emma's Waltz*, *Autumn in the Valley*, *Dream of the Manatee* (with Joe Weed), and *Oktober County*, all on the Gourd Music label.

In collaboration with Joe Weed, Neal wrote the score for *Princess Furball*, a children's video by Weston Woods which won a 1993 American Library Association Commendation.

An original composition, written by Neal and performed by Jay Unger and Molly Mason, is featured on the Ken Burns production "The Story of Susan B. Anthony and Elizabeth Cady Stanton," which was broadcasted on PBS nationwide in the fall of 1999.

He is the author of many books on the Appalachian dulcimer, including *Celtic Songs & Slow Airs for Mountain Dulcimer*, *The Dulcimer Chord Book*, *The Hal Leonard Dulcimer Method*, *Hits of the Beatles Dulcimer Book* and *The Music of the Shakers For Mountain Dulcimer*.

As founder, director, and one of the primary artists of the Gourd Music record label, Neal has produced over 40 albums, including *Simple Gifts*, *Tree of Life*, *The Fairie Round*, *Tender Shepherd*, *The World Turned Upside Down*, and *Celtic Sessions*, creating a uniquely distinctive sound, featuring a variety of acoustic instrumental ensembles, rich in texture and tonal color.

He recently worked as musical director for a production of *The Grapes of Wrath*, which was performed at Cabrillo College in November of 2009.

INTRODUCTION

Many years have passed since I sat by an oil lamp in a hiker's cabin in British Columbia and wrote my first book, *Life Is Like a Mountain Dulcimer*. I remember sitting in that drafty cabin writing the first draft. I wrote that book from the viewpoint of a student learning how to play the dulcimer. Many books, a number of albums, and countless workshops later, I have the opportunity to give you the benefit of my experience in a new beginner's method for the dulcimer.

In the past few decades of teaching workshops throughout the United States, I have seen an incredible change in dulcimer playing through the efforts of the present generation of dulcimer teachers. Many new approaches are being taken to enhance the instrument. In addition to its melodic style, folks are now seeing what a versatile "rhythm" or "back-up" instrument the dulcimer can be.

The Hal Leonard Dulcimer Method will give you a solid grounding in technique and teach you how the instrument works. You will learn a wide variety of interesting dulcimer solos and how to accompany your voice or other instruments. By the end of the book, you will discover how this versatile instrument can add great enjoyment to your life.

ACKNOWLEDGMENTS

Special thanks to Phyllis Dunne for the section on fingerpicking, Kim Robertson for teaching me many of the tunes, Craig Johnson, William Coulter for help with the arrangements, Barry Phillips, Janet Herman, Will Schmid for editing the first version, Cathy Lenox for proofreading, and Hal Leonard Corporation for editing the second edition of this book.

YOUR DULCIMER

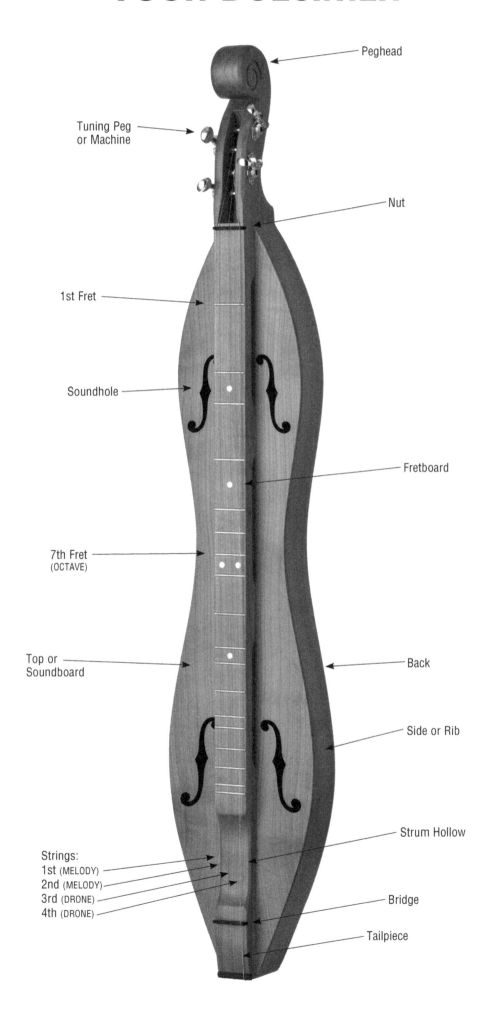

Peghead

Tuning Peg or Machine

Nut

1st Fret

Soundhole

Fretboard

7th Fret (OCTAVE)

Top or Soundboard

Back

Side or Rib

Strum Hollow

Strings:
1st (MELODY)
2nd (MELODY)
3rd (DRONE)
4th (DRONE)

Bridge

Tailpiece

HOLDING THE DULCIMER

First, find yourself a chair you're comfortable in. Place the dulcimer on your lap. Does it slide off? Many of my students who have short legs place something under their feet. If you have a hard shell dulcimer case, this will do fine. The best cure for a sliding dulcimer is to install strap pegs and a strap. If you feel unsure about this, ask someone at your local music store. For a small fee, I'm sure they will install them for you. For a strap, any guitar strap will do. Be sure to keep the buckle in a place where you can adjust the strap. If you drew a line from your navel it should come out around the 9th fret. I've found this to be an optimal placement when starting. Experiment with placement. Some folks like it close to their body, on an angle, or positioned so they can play the instrument from over the top. Find out what works best for you.

TUNING

As you progress through this method, you will learn many ways to tune a dulcimer. Let's start with a favorite among many dulcimer players, DD–A–D.

TUNING TO A PIANO

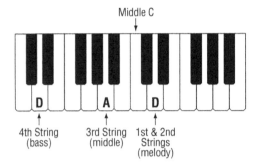

Carefully locate which tuning peg goes with each string before loosening or tightening the string.

You know you are in tune when the two sounds merge into one sound. If you turn the peg and the pitches get further apart, you are turning the wrong way.

TUNING THE DULCIMER TO ITSELF

- Tune the bass string to where it's not too loose or too tight (to a D, using a piano as a reference).

- Press the bass string to the left of the 4th fret and tune the open middle string to this note.

- Press the bass string to the left of the 7th fret and tune one of the open melody strings to this note.

- Using the tuned 1st string, tune the other unison string to this note.

NOTE: If you're having trouble, remember it is easiest to start at a lower pitch and tune up to the desired note.

This tuning should give a nice even sound (sort of like bagpipes) when the open strings are strummed. Check your tuning often; you'll enjoy playing more when it's in tune. If you have wooden "friction" pegs, try pushing in while tuning. If they still creak badly, go to a fiddle shop and buy some "peg dope;" ask the fiddle person for advice on putting it on.

TUNING TO AN ELECTRONIC TUNER

If tuning is a real problem for you, an electronic tuner will greatly help. You will be able to tune "by sight"—that is, let a needle/dial tell you when you are in tune.

GETTING STARTED

I know how anxious you must be to get started. I have picked out a few tunes you can play without any theory. However, there are some things I want to convey that will greatly aid you in playing the first few tunes.

READING THE TABLATURE

At the top of each tune is the title. Usually there is a little instruction or explanation under the title. You will next see a standard five-line musical staff. See page 77 for "Music Symbols Used in This Book." (This book will not teach you how to read music.) Lyrics are included if the tune is also a ballad.

Below the five-line staff are three lines with numbers written on the lines. This is the tablature, or tab, staff. The bottom line represents the first string or first pair of strings, the middle line represents the middle string, and the top line represents the bass string. The numbers on the lines represent the fret at which you push down to "stop" the string and thus create a note. Most of the melodies in the book are played on the first string or pair of strings.

Many of the tunes have back-up chord letters written above the musical staff. Next to each chord letter are three numbers:

$$\text{Gm} \quad \begin{matrix} 3 & \Longleftarrow & \textbf{bass string} \\ 0 & \Longleftarrow & \textbf{middle string} \\ 4 & \Longleftarrow & \textbf{unison or treble strings} \end{matrix}$$

The numbers represent the frets. To play this Gm chord, strum across all the strings while pressing the 4th fret of the treble strings and the 3rd fret of the bass string. The middle string is left open (not fretted).

FRETTING (THE LEFT HAND)

Always fret directly to the *left* of the desired fret (see photo). Fret with the tip of your finger or with the side of your thumb.

THE PICK

Pick choice is an individual matter. Go to your local music store, where there is an ample supply of picks, and try out all you can. You want a pick that's firm enough so it won't sound floppy, yet not so hard that it will impede your strumming.

Hold the pick between your thumb and index finger, but don't tense up. It's better to have the pick fly out from your hand than to hold it too tightly. If you hold the pick too tightly, you will tense up your entire wrist and arm and greatly hurt your strumming ability.

Holding the pick

Strumming away from you (⊓)…

…and back (V) across the strings

PICK ANGLE

You might want to accent a certain string. With the melody on the treble string, you must angle your pick so you won't drown the melody out. The same is true when your melody is on the bass string.

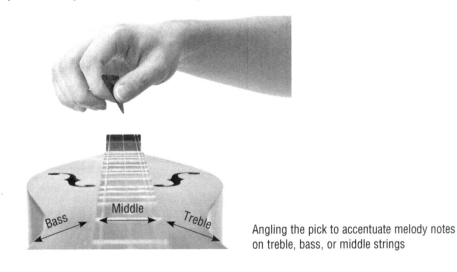

Angling the pick to accentuate melody notes on treble, bass, or middle strings

MR. MELLOW AND MR. BITE

The closer to the bridge you strum or pick, the more bite the sound will have. The farther from the bridge you strum, the more mellow the instrument will sound.

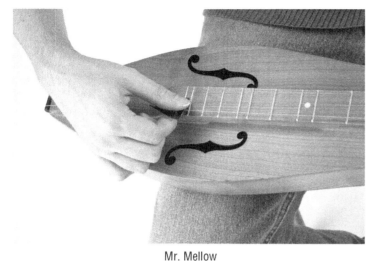

Mr. Mellow

Mr. Bite

RIGHT HAND STRUMMING

I have always found rhythm the hardest to teach. There are no "set" patterns. Each song, tune, or dance seems to require a different pattern from the one before.

To show you some basic strum patterns, let's use these two symbols:

      ◻ = strum away from you

      V = strum back toward you

Now for a start, just strum away from your body (◻). Relax, and don't tense up. Be aware of how you are holding the pick (mellow and bite) and how you're striking the instrument.

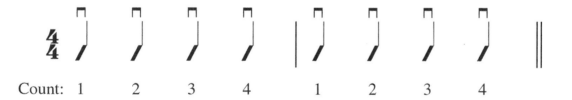

Now add the up (return) strum (V) between each count.

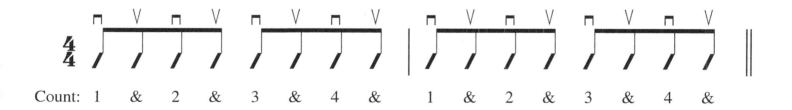

Here are two more common strums in $\frac{4}{4}$ time:

Two ways of strumming in $\frac{3}{4}$ or waltz time are:

A typical strum pattern for a $\frac{6}{8}$ jig might be:

FIRST SONGS

Let's start by strumming "When the Saints Go Marching In." It was often sung in New Orleans on the way back from a funeral. It's a happy song because the soul was now on the way home, and everyone was glad. Start with spirit and energy. Let's not worry about modes and keys just yet; let's play the rhythm version.

- Start by strumming just the open strings. Tap your foot. Do you feel awkward? Pause for a moment and start again. Begin with any away strum (◼); then when you feel more confident, add the return strum (V).

- The chord fingerings are suggestions. Many folks don't like to use their thumb, so find out what works best for you. Abbreviations are:

t = thumb, i = index, m = middle, and r = ring finger

- In the melody version, be sure you are angling your pick so as not to drown out the melody (see page 8). Go back and forth between the melody version and the rhythm version. In this tuning (DD–A–D), you can play the melody on the bass string using the same fret numbers. The only difference is that it will be an octave lower. If you'd like to hear a high pitched version, start on the 7th fret of the melody strings. In other words, add 7 to all your fret numbers. Your melody is still the same, but now it's an octave higher.

"Little Moses" is a wonderful old Carter Family tune and a favorite of mine. This is 3/4 time, or waltz time. So let's count 1, 2, 3, 1, 2, 3, 1, 2, 3.

- The 1/0/1 chord is played in the melody version to enhance the sound of the piece. Note that this time the chord names and fingerings are written above the musical staff.

- Don't try to sing when you play the melody. Use the chords to accompany your voice. Use the melody as a break from singing to let yourself or a listener enjoy the "voice" of the dulcimer. Remember, take it nice and slow, counting as you strum:

1, 2, 3, 1, 2, 3, 1, 2, 3

WHEN THE SAINTS GO MARCHING IN
(Rhythm Version)

Before playing the rhythm version of "When the Saints Go Marching In," practice strumming the chords below. The left-handed fingering is only a suggestion (t = thumb, i = index, m = middle, and r = ring finger); feel free to change it to suit yourself.

Sing and strum the chords for this rhythm version of "When the Saints Go Marching In." Begin with an away strum (⊓) on each beat; then try the away/return strum given at the bottom of page 9.

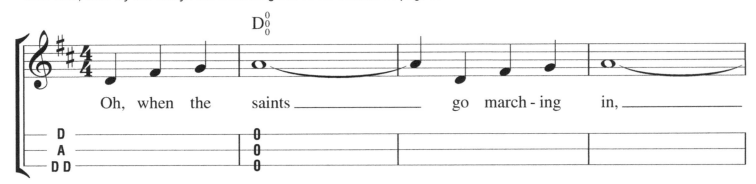

Oh, when the saints _____ go march - ing in, _____

_____ oh, when the saints go march - ing in. _____

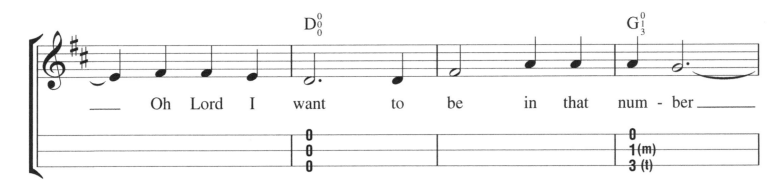

_____ Oh Lord I want to be in that num - ber _____

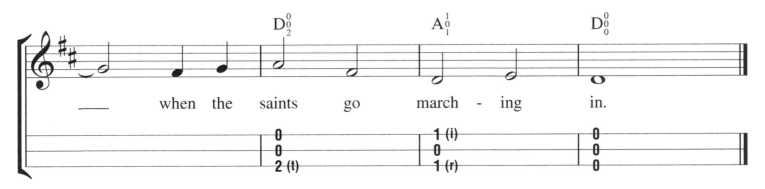

_____ when the saints go march - ing in.

ALTERNATE CHORD FINGERINGS: D   G   A

12

WHEN THE SAINTS GO MARCHING IN
(Melody Version)

Run your finger(s) along the 1st (melody) string(s) and press at the frets indicated by the numbers. Strum across all of the strings, but finger only the first strings. The middle and bass strings will sound like a bagpipe drone.

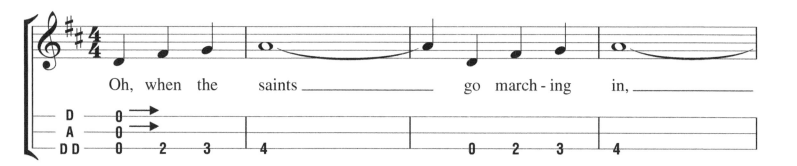

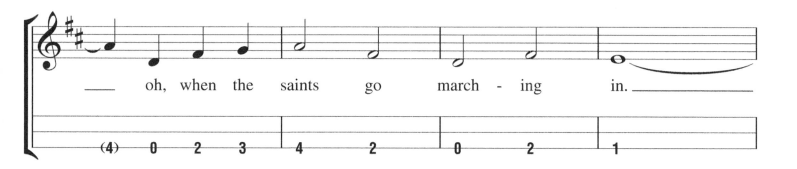

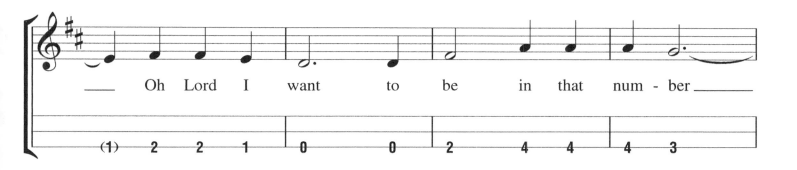

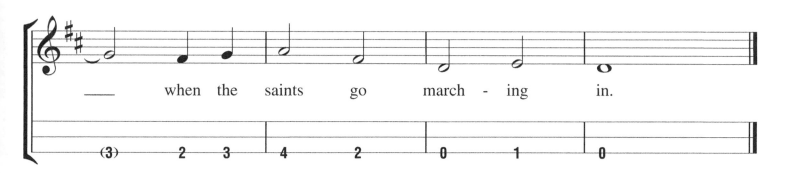

LITTLE MOSES

In "Little Moses," you will find both the chords for the rhythm part (above the staff) and the melody tab. In the third phrase, the melody is doubled on the bass string as well. First practice the melody, then the chords, strumming three times per measure.

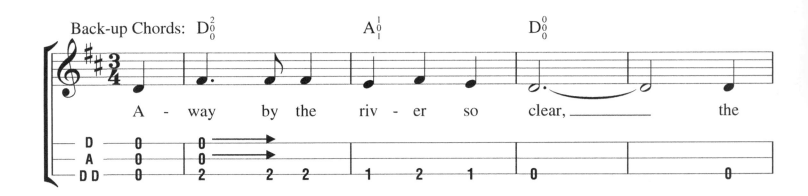

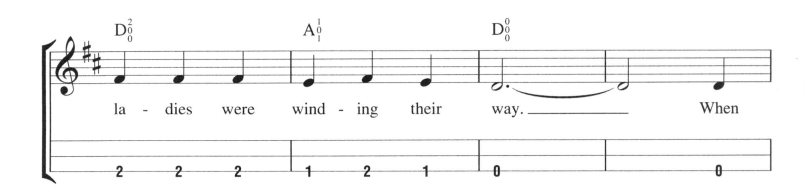

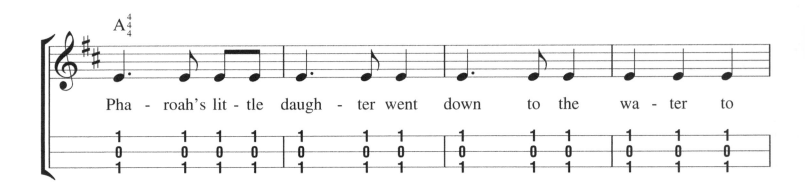

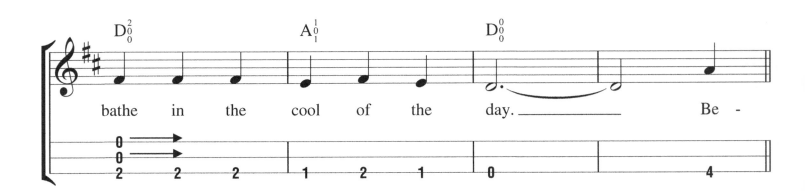

fore   it   was   dark,   she   o - pened   the   ark   and

found   the sweet   in - fant   was   there. _____   Be - ___

D A D	D A D

2. And away by the waters so blue,

        A   **D**
The infant was lonely and sad.

   A
She took him in pity and thought him so pretty,

   D   **A**   **D**
And it made little Moses so glad.

        G **D**   **G D**
She called him her own, her beautiful son

        A   **D**
And sent for a nurse that was near.

        D   **A**   **D**
3. And away by the river so clear,

        A   **D**
They carried the beautiful child

   A
To his own tender mother, his sister, and brother,

   D   **A**   **D**
Little Moses looked happy and smiled.

        G **D**   **G D**
His mother so good did all that she could

        A   **D**
To rear him and teach him with care.

4. And away by the sea that was red,

        A   **D**
Little Moses the servant of God,

   A
While in him confided, the sea was divided,

   D   **A**   **D**
As upward he lifted his rod.

        G D   **G D**
The Jews stepped across while Pharoah's host

        A   **D**
Was drowned in the waters and lost.

        D   **A**   **D**
5. And away on the mountain so high,

        A   **D**
The last one that he might see,

   A
While in Him victorious, his hope was most glorious,

   D   **A**   **D**
That soon all Jordan be free.

        G D   **G D**
When his labors did cease, he departed in peace,

        A   **D**
And rested in the heavens above.

JOHN HARDY

Begin "John Hardy" by playing the melody on the treble string(s); then play the easy chord version, which uses an open D chord in measures 1–3 and 5–9. When you are feeling more adventuresome, try the chords given in measures 1–3.

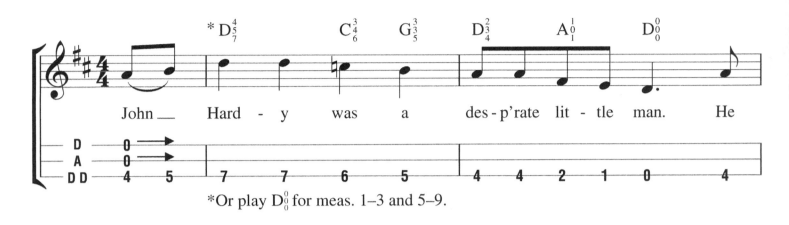

*Or play D_0^0 for meas. 1–3 and 5–9.

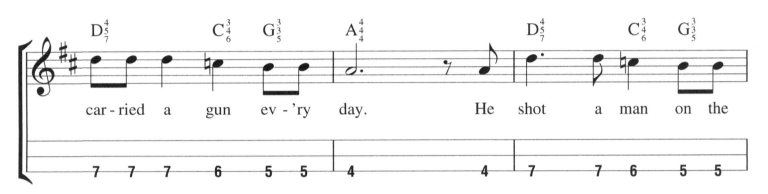

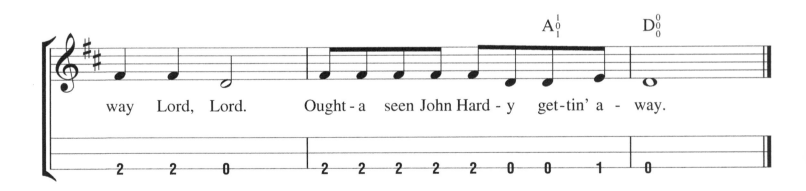

              D   (C   G   D   A) D
2. John Hardy stood in that old bar room
       D   (C   G) A
    So drunk that he could not see.
        D   (C G D   A)   D
    And a man walked up and took him by the arm;
    D
    He said, "Johnny, come and go along with me,
                            A   D
    Poor boy, Johnny, come and walk along with me."

       D   (C   G   D A) D
3. John Hardy stood in his old jail cell,
        D   (C   G)   A
    The tears running down from his eyes.
        D   (C   G   D A) D
    He said, "I've been the death of many a poor boy,
    D
    But my six shooters never told a lie,
                      A   D
    No, my six shooters never told a lie."

        D   (C G D   A)   D
4. The first one to visit John Hardy in his cell
        D   (C   G) A
    Was a little girl dressed in blue.
        D   (C G D A) D
    She came down to that old jail cell;
    D
    She said, "Johnny, I've been true to you.
                         A   D
    God knows, Johnny, I've been true to you."

             D   (C   G   D   A) D
5. The next one to visit John Hardy in his cell
              D   (C   G) A
    Was a little girl dressed in red.
    D   (C   G   D A) D
    She came down to that old jail cell;
    D
    She said, "Johnny, I had rather see you dead,
                        A   D
    Well, Johnny, I had rather see you dead."

           D   (C G   D   A)   D
6. "I've been to the East and I've been to the West,
           D   (C   G)   A
    I've traveled this wide world around;
         D   (C   G   D   A)   D
    I've been to the river and I've been baptized,
    D
    So take me to my burying ground,
                       A   D
    So take me to my burying ground."

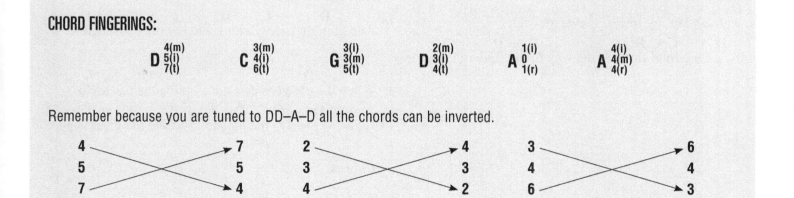

THE LARK IN THE MORNING

Here's another fun tune to practice.

D   G   A
2. Lay still my fond shepherd and don't you rise yet,
      D   C   D   A D
   It's a fine dewy morning, and besides, me love it is wet.

      D   G   A
3. Oh let it be wet my love and ever so cold,
      D   C   D   A D
   I will rise me fond flora on the way to my fold.

Chorus Oh the lark in the morning, she rises from her nest,

             D   G   A

              D   C   D   A D
And she mounts in the air with the dew on her breast.
             D   G   A
And like the pretty plowboy, she'll whistle and sing,
             D   C   D   A D
And at night she will return to her own nest again.

             D   G   A
4. When the plowboy has done all that he has to do,
             D   C   D   A D
He trips down to the meadows where the grass is all cut down

Chorus

18

THE MIXOLYDIAN AND IONIAN MODES

To play in the following modes, tune your dulcimer as indicated below.

MIXOLYDIAN MODE

This is the tuning you have already been using.

— Tune the bass string to D.

— Press the bass string to the left of the 4th fret, and tune the open middle string to this note (A).

— Press the bass string to the left of the 7th fret, and tune the treble or unison strings to this note (DD).

You may tune to C if you wish, but remember the tunes in this chapter are written out in D. Traditional music is more likely to be played in D rather than in C.

The scale starts on the open unison strings and goes up to the 7th fret.

DD–A–D (Key of D)

IONIAN MODE

— Tune the bass string to D.

— Press the bass string to the left of the 3rd fret, and tune the open middle string to this note (G).

— Press the bass string to the left of the 7th fret, and tune the open melody strings to this note (D).

DD–G–D (Key of G)

The Ionian mode, also known as the major scale, starts on the 3rd fret (melody strings) and goes to the 10th fret. As with the Mixolydian tuning, the melody can be played on both the treble and bass strings. You will find that a lot of traditional music is played in G.

You now have two major tunings in two different keys. All you need to do to change from one to another is tune the middle string up or down one whole step.

Later in the book, we will explore playing an Ionian scale in the DD–A–D tuning by using the extra 6½ fret.

Please don't ignore the "back-up" chords. Accompanying a tune or a ballad is as important as playing the melody. The back-up chords will help your rhythm and make it easier to sing your favorite ballad.

A **mode** is a sequence of tones and semi-tones that forms a musical scale. What differentiates one mode from another is the various combinations of tones and semi-tones. A mode is *not* a key. A **key** refers to the **tonic** (starting) note of a particular scale or mode.

Take, for example, our first tuning: DD–A–D. If you start on the open note (treble string) and play each fret up to and including the 7th fret, you have the following:

Note:	D	E	F#	G	A	B	C	D
Fret #:	Open	1	2	3	4	5	6	7

This is the D Mixolydian mode. Why? It's because of the following combination of steps and half steps (tones and semi-tones):

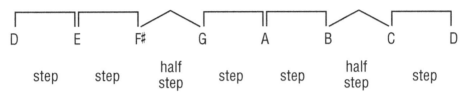

Another way to cite the Mixolydian mode is:

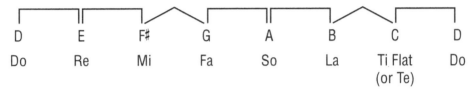

The Mixolydian mode is like a major scale with a lowered 7th note. No matter what key you are in (C, D, E, F, etc.) the Mixolydian mode is always characterized by the particular combination of:

step – step – ½ step – step – step – ½ step

The Mixolydian is one of three major-sounding modes. The flatted 7th gives it kind of a "bluesy" tint. "John Henry," "John Hardy," "Don't Let Your Deal Go Down," and "The Lark in the Morning" are all in this mode. Many laments from the British Isles are in the Mixolydian, the flatted 7th adding a poignant characteristic to a ballad like "Flowers of the Forest."

Another major-sounding mode used a lot more in Western music is the Ionian or major scale. The Ionian is like the Mixolydian except it does not have a flatted 7th. Still in our DD–A–D tuning, place one of your fingers on the 3rd fret, middle string. Now play all the notes up to and including the 10th. You have just played the following:

Note:	D	E	F#	G	A	B	C#	D
Fret #: (on middle string)	3	4	5	6	7	8	9	10

Notice the notes are the same as before except for the 7th. We now have a C# and not a C♮. Here's the Ionian in terms of steps and half steps:

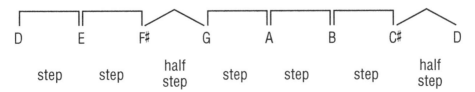

Another way to view the Ionian:

D	E	F♯	G	A	B	C♯	D
Do	Re	Mi	Fa	So	La	<u>Ti</u>	Do

Tunes like "Three Jolly Rogues of Lynn," "Arkansas Traveler," and many, many more are in the Ionian mode.

REVIEW

- A mode is a sequence of tones and semi-tones (steps and half steps) within a musical scale.

- A mode is not a key.

- The steps and half steps within a particular mode will always be the same, regardless of the key.

- The Mixolydian mode differs from the Ionian (major) in that the Mixolydian has a flatted 7th.

What is the mode of a tune in a major key if the 7th note in the scale doesn't occur in the tune? Look back on the first two compositions we played ("Little Moses" and "Saints"). Neither of these tunes has a 7th note (C or C♯ in this case). Therefore, they are not in either mode and can be played while tuned to the Mixolydian or the Ionian. "Twinkle, Twinkle," "London Bridge," and "My Home's Across the Smokey Mountains" are all tunes that have no 7th note and therefore can be played in either mode. Be aware of this; it will help you later on when you start learning from books other than dulcimer books.

How will all this information help you as a dulcimer player, you might ask? Say you open a book of American folk tunes. This book has just a standard musical staff. There are two sharps (♯) written on the staff. This means the tune is in D. However, you see that in front of every C note there is a natural sign (♮). This will tell you (if you know your modes) to tune to the Mixolydian to play the piece. Why? Simple: all the C♯ notes are now (C) naturals, which means a flatted 7th (Mixolydian mode). If there are no C naturals, then the tune is in Ionian.

Your first Mixolydian tune, "John Hardy," was in the key of D with the dulcimer tuned DD–A–D. If you'd rather play it in the key of C—just turn all the strings down one whole step to CC–G–C. Now you can play all the same fret numbers indicated for the melody and the back up chords. Why? Because for a given mode, the sequence of tones and semi-tones (steps and half steps) is the same for any key.

Please don't try to digest all this information at once. Try playing some of the Mixolydian tunes, then some of the Ionian tunes, and listen carefully. You'll soon be able to hear that telltale 7th note and will be on your way to truly understanding what the instrument is all about. In time, this knowledge will help you arrange and compose your own music, and give you the ability to teach yourself.

THE FLOWERS OF THE FOREST

This is a Scottish lament based on the defeat of Bonny Prince Charlie to the English at Culloden-Moor in 1745. Since this is a slow lament, try using all up (V) strokes.

2. Sad day for the orders that sent them to the border,
The English by guile for once won the day.
Now they are mourning, for all times lamenting,
The flowers of the forest are all wede away.

3. I've heard them lilting all at the ewes a-milkin'
And I've heard them lilting before light of day.
Now they are mourning for all times lamenting,
The flowers of the forest are all wede away.

SUGGESTED FINGERINGS:

THUGAMAR FÉIN AN SAMHRADH LINN
(We Brought the Summer with Us)

Try also playing this ancient Irish melody on the bass string.

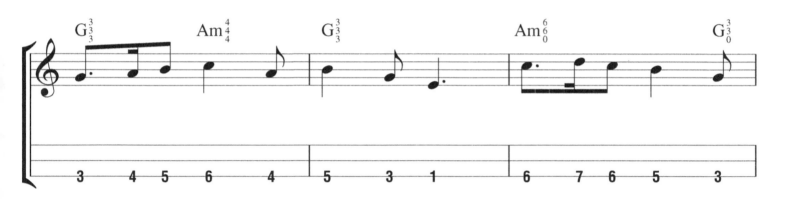

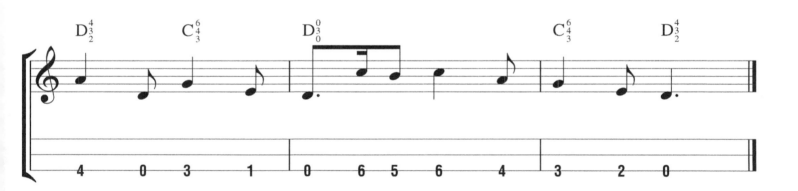

THREE JOLLY ROGUES OF LYNN

Try out this English folk song in G Ionian.

    G   **D**   **G**
2. Now the miller, he stole corn.
    G   **D** **G**
    And the weaver, he stole yarn.
         D   **Em**   **Bm**
    And the little tailor, he stole broadcloth
     C   **D**   **G**
    For to keep these three rogues warm.
        C   **G**
    For to keep these three rogues warm,
        C   **G**
    For to keep these three rogues warm,
        D   **Em**   **Bm**
    And the little tailor, he stole broadcloth
     C   **D**   **G**
    For to keep these three rogues warm.

    G   **D**   **G**
3. Now the miller got drowned in his dam,
   G   **D**   **G**
    The weaver got hung in his yarn,
        D   **Em**   **Bm**
    And the devil put his claw on the little trailor
     C   **D**   **G**
    With the broadcloth under his arm.
        C   **G**
    With the broadcloth under his arm,
        C   **G**
    With the broadcloth under his arm,
        D   **Em**   **Bm**
    And the devil put his claw on the little trailor
     C   **D**   **G**
    With the broadcloth under his arm.

    G   **D**   **G**
4. Now the miller still drowns in his dam,
    G   **D**   **G**
    And the weaver still hangs in his yarn,
        D   **Em**   **Bm**
    And the little tailor goes a-skippin' thru hell
     C   **D**   **G**
    With the broadcloth under his arm.
        C   **G**
    With the broadcloth under his arm,
        C   **G**
    With the broadcloth under his arm,
        D   **Em**   **Bm**
    And the little tailor goes a-skippin' thru hell
     C   **D**   **G**
    With the broadcloth under his arm.

5. Repeat first verse

THE BABY TREE

Start by singing with the back-up chords. The melody can also be played on the bass string: remember to "angle" your pick.

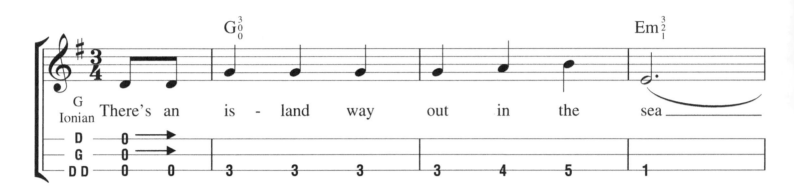

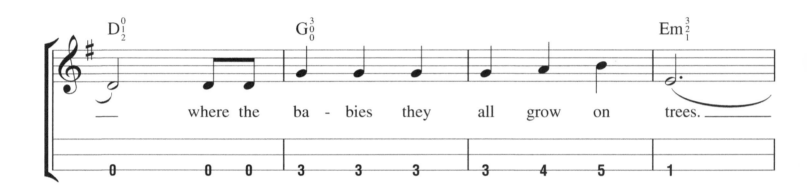

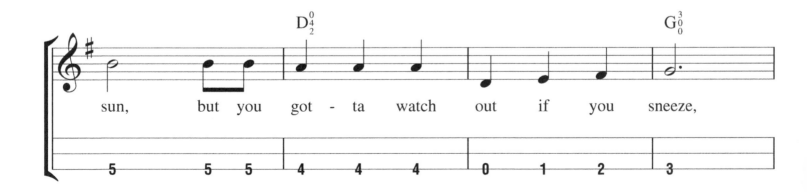

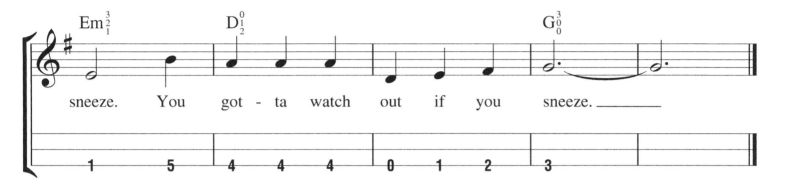

sneeze.   You   got - ta   watch   out   if   you   sneeze. _____

          G   **Em** **D**
2. Now you gotta watch out if you sneeze
          G   **Em** **D**
  For a-hanging way up in the trees.
         C
  You just might cough
         G
  And they will fall off,
  D   **G**   **Em**
  Tumble down flop on your knees, knees.
  D   **G**
  Tumble down flop on your knees.

          G   **Em D**
3. Now when the stormy wind wail
          G   **Em D**
  And the breakers blow up on a gale
         C   **G**
  There's various flopping, and dropping,

  and plopping.
  D   **G**   **Em**
  Fat little babies just hail, hail.
  D   **G**
  Fat little babies just hail.

          G   **Em D**
4. Now the babies fall into a pile,
          G   **Em D**
  And the grown-ups come after a while.
         C
  And they always pass by
         G
  The babies that cry,
  D   **G**   **Em**
  Take only babies that smile, smile,
  D   **G**
  Triplets and twins if they smile.

SUGGESTED FINGERING: Em $^{3(i)}_{2(m)}_{1(r)}$

THE GIRL I LEFT BEHIND ME

Try using all your fingers. Start with your i, m, and r over the 10, 9, 8 frets, respectively.

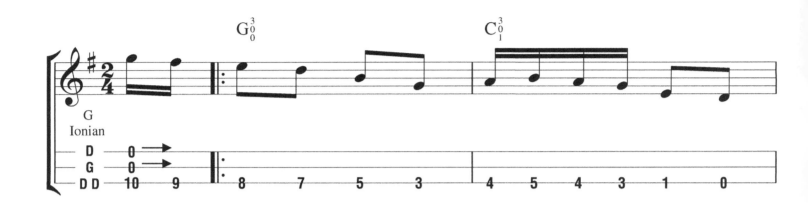

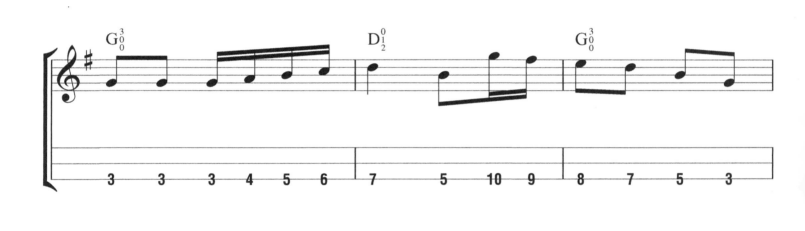

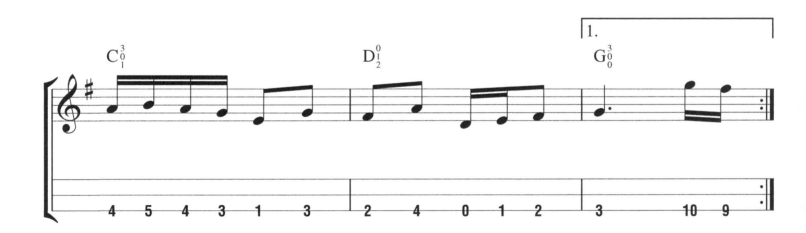

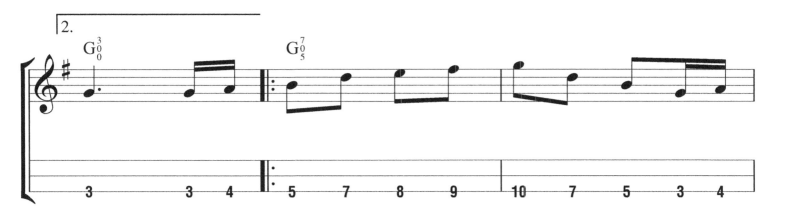

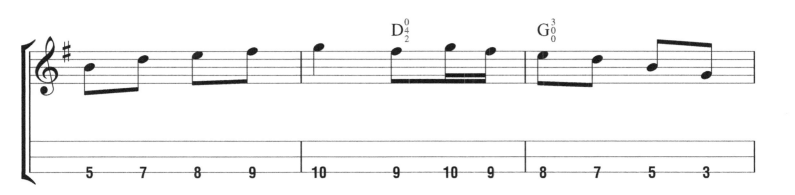

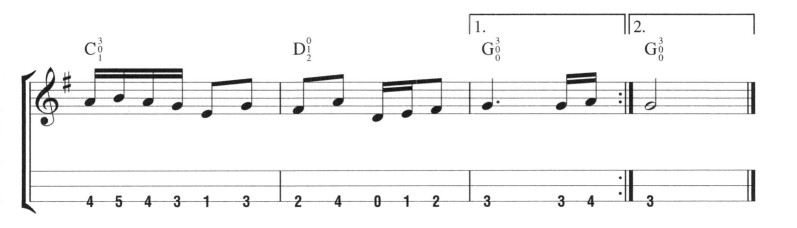

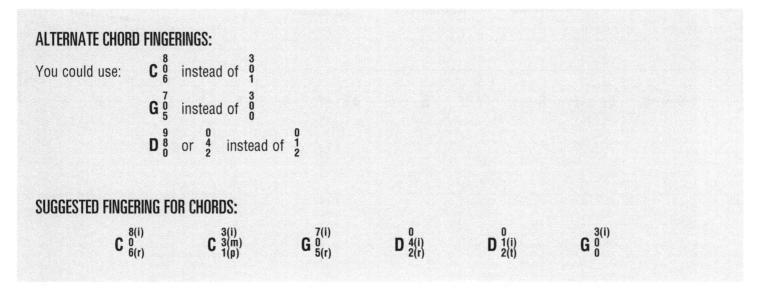

ALTERNATE CHORD FINGERINGS:

You could use:
$C \begin{smallmatrix} 8 \\ 0 \\ 6 \end{smallmatrix}$ instead of $\begin{smallmatrix} 3 \\ 0 \\ 1 \end{smallmatrix}$

$G \begin{smallmatrix} 7 \\ 0 \\ 5 \end{smallmatrix}$ instead of $\begin{smallmatrix} 3 \\ 0 \\ 0 \end{smallmatrix}$

$D \begin{smallmatrix} 9 \\ 8 \\ 0 \end{smallmatrix}$ or $\begin{smallmatrix} 0 \\ 4 \\ 2 \end{smallmatrix}$ instead of $\begin{smallmatrix} 0 \\ 1 \\ 2 \end{smallmatrix}$

SUGGESTED FINGERING FOR CHORDS:

$C \begin{smallmatrix} 8(i) \\ 0 \\ 6(r) \end{smallmatrix}$ $\quad$ $C \begin{smallmatrix} 3(i) \\ 3(m) \\ 1(p) \end{smallmatrix}$ $\quad$ $G \begin{smallmatrix} 7(i) \\ 0 \\ 5(r) \end{smallmatrix}$ $\quad$ $D \begin{smallmatrix} 0 \\ 4(i) \\ 2(r) \end{smallmatrix}$ $\quad$ $D \begin{smallmatrix} 0 \\ 1(i) \\ 2(t) \end{smallmatrix}$ $\quad$ $G \begin{smallmatrix} 3(i) \\ 0 \\ 0 \end{smallmatrix}$

THE IRISH WASHERWOMAN

Remember a great advantage of the Ionian mode is that you can play the melody on the bass string as well as the treble. For those hard stretches on these next two songs, use your ring finger and thumb.

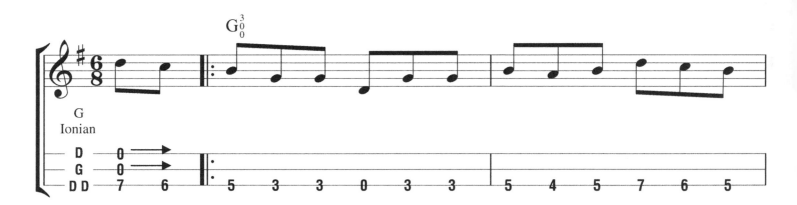

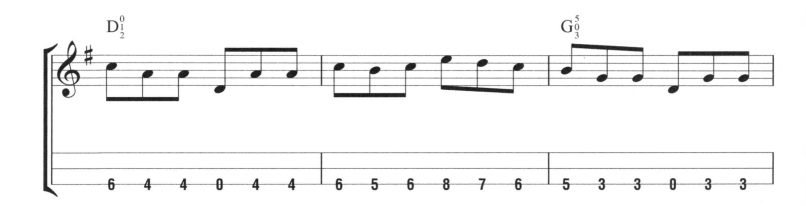

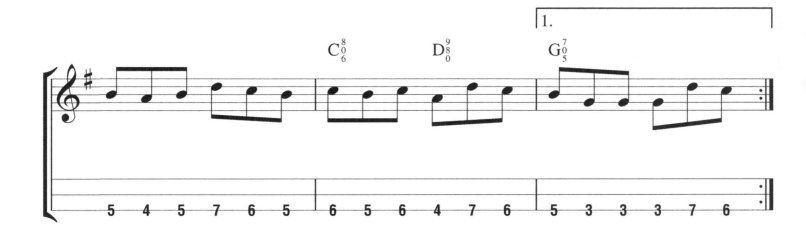

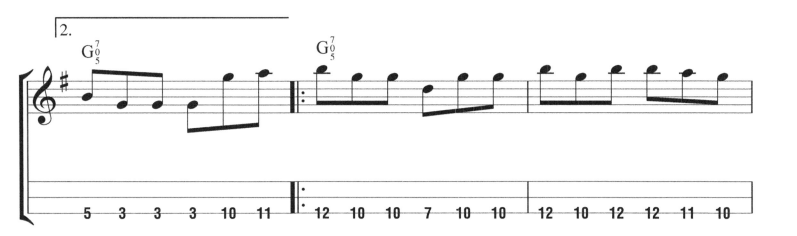

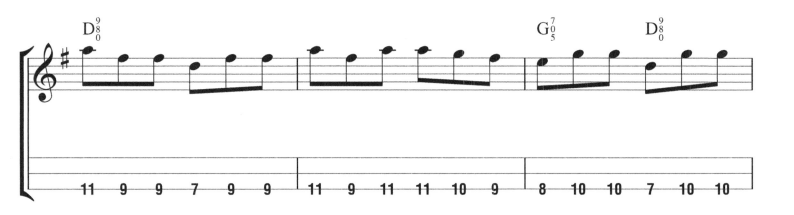

SCOTLAND THE BRAVE

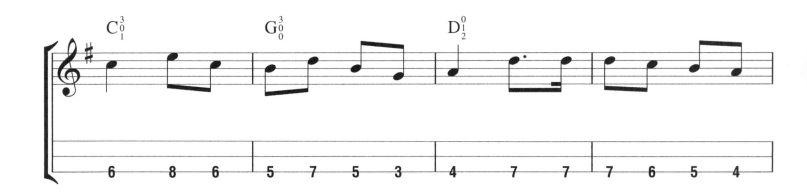

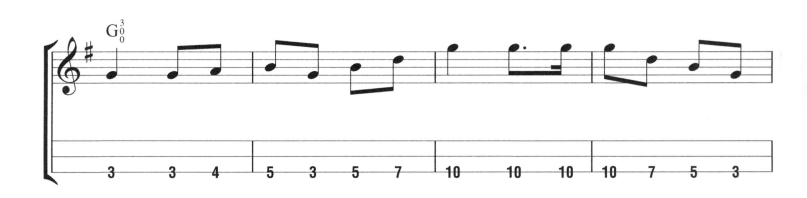

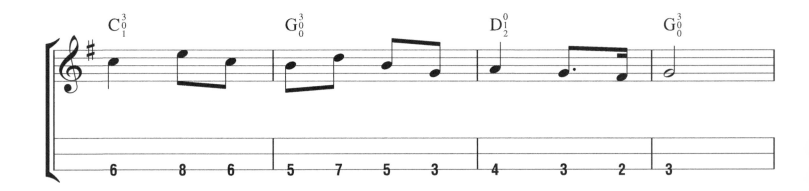

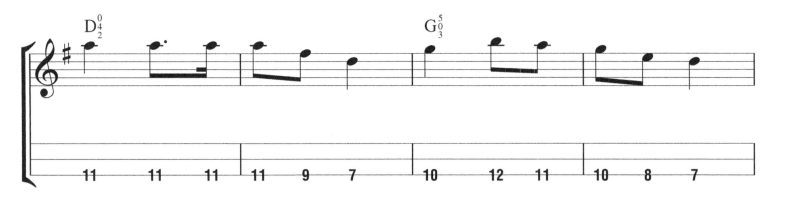

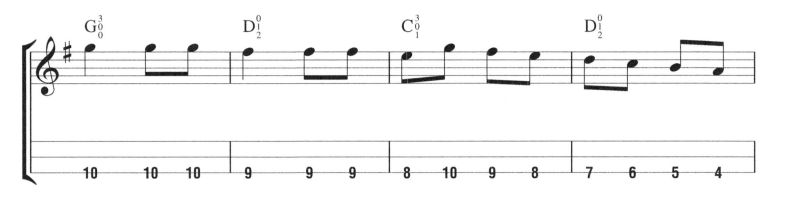

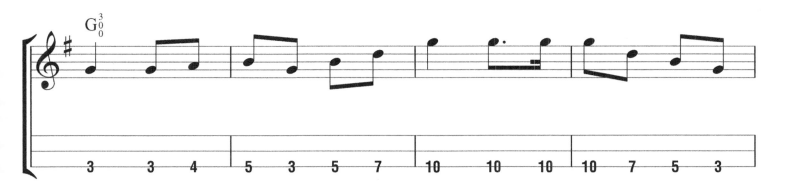

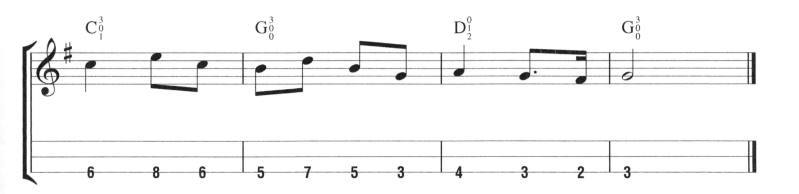

SPOTTED COW

A simple down-up-down-up-down-up pattern is best to back up this humorous English ballad. Keep your wrist loose and relaxed while you play. Let the rhythm take care of itself while you concentrate on the vocal part. Note also that you are tuned DD–A–D, yet the vocal part is Ionian.

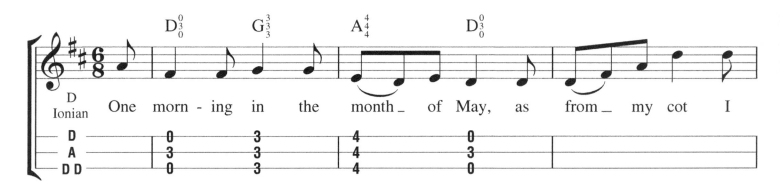

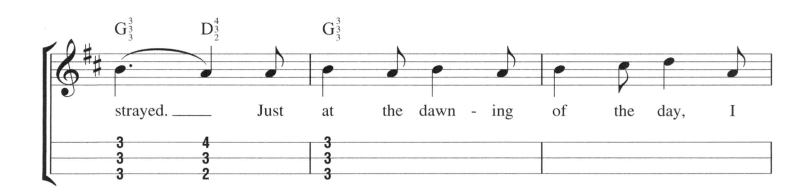

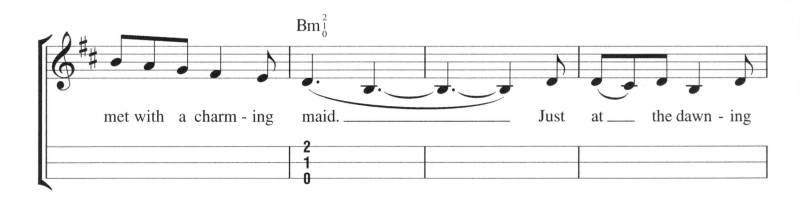

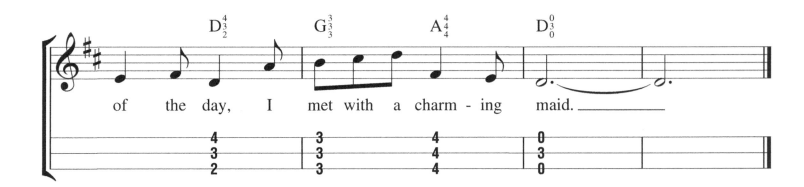

     D   **G**   **A**   **D**
2. "Good morning to you" whither said I,
                  G   **D**
"Good morning to you now."
    G
The maid replied, "kind sir," she cried,
        Bm
"I've lost me spotted cow."
                  D
The maid replied, "kind sir," she cried,
     G   **A**   **D**
"I've lost me spotted cow."

      D   **G**   **A**   **D**
3. No longer weep, no longer mourn.
             G   **D**
Your cow's not lost, my dear.
 G
I saw her down in yonder grove;
           Bm
Come, love, and I'll show you where.
         D
I saw her down in yonder grove;
   G   **A**   **D**
Come, love, and I'll show you where."

     D   **G**   **A** **D**
4. "I must confess, you're very kind.
             G **D**
I thank you, sire," she said.
   G
"We will be sure her there to find.
           Bm
Come, love, and I'll show you where.
         D
We will be sure her there to find.
   G   **A**   **D**
Come, love, and I'll show you where."

     D   **G**   **A**   **D**
5. And in the grove they spent the day.
                    G   **D**
The thought it passed too soon.
    G
At night they homeward bent their way
         Bm
While brightly shone the moon.
                   D
At night they homeward bent their way
    G   **A**   **D**
While brightly shone the moon.

     D   **G**   **A**   **D**
6. If he should cross the flowery dale
                G   **D**
Or go to view the plow,
    G
She comes and calls, "you gentle swain,
         Bm
I've lost me spotted cow."
                   D
She comes and calls, "you gentle swain,
    G   **A**   **D**
I've lost me spotted cow."

SUGGESTED FINGERING FOR CHORDS:

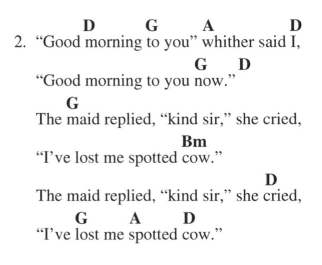

THE MARCH OF THE KING OF LAOIS

Another Mixolydian tuning is AA–A–A. From DD–A–D, tune your treble and bass strings down to match the open middle string. If you wish you can play in DD–A–D, the fret numbers will be the same, but the key will be D.

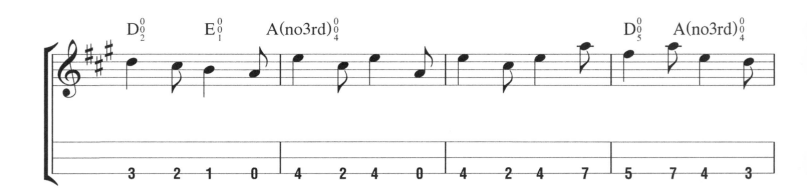

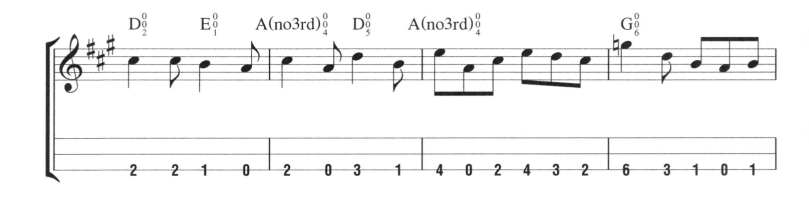

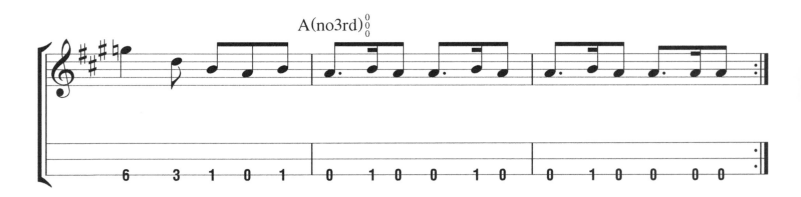

THE AEOLIAN AND DORIAN MODES

The two minor modes you will be playing in are the Aeolian (also known as the minor scale) and the Dorian.

AEOLIAN MODE

— Tune bass string to D.

— Press bass string to the left of the 4th fret, and tune the open middle string to this note.

— Press bass string to the left of the 6th fret, and tune the open melody strings to this note.

CC–A–D (Key of D minor)

In this tuning, the Aeolian mode starts on the first fret (melody strings) and goes to the 8th fret. The Aeolian mode is characterized by a flatted 3rd, 6th, and 7th as compared to the Ionian.

DORIAN MODE

— Tune the bass string to D.

— Press bass string to the left of the 3rd fret, and tune the open middle string to this note.

— Press bass string to the left of the 6th fret, and tune open treble strings to this note.

CC–G–D (Key of G minor)

Dorian is basically the Aeolian mode with a raised 6th.

ANOTHER DORIAN TUNING

— Tune to the Mixolydian DD–A–D.

— Drop the bass string way down to match the open middle string.

DD–A–A (Key of A minor)

The Dorian mode will start on the 4th fret (treble string) and end on the 11th fret.

The difference between the Aeolian and Dorian modes is the 6th note. If a tune is in a minor key and has no 6th ("Shady Grove," "None-Such," etc.) then it can be played in either tuning. A composition such as "God Rest Ye Merry Gentlemen" or "The Cuckoo," which have a flatted 6th, would have to be played in the Aeolian tuning; "Tralee Jail" and "Wraggle-Taggle Gypsies" have a natural 6th and would therefore be played in Dorian.

In a later section of the book, you will learn how to play in the Dorian mode while tuned to the Aeolian by using the "extra" (6½) fret.

HATIKVA

Listen to how the flatted 6th (C) adds to the color of this beautiful song from the Middle East.

THE MOON SHINES BRIGHT

For this arrangement, you will use the flatpick to articulate single notes as well as full strums. Play what you see.

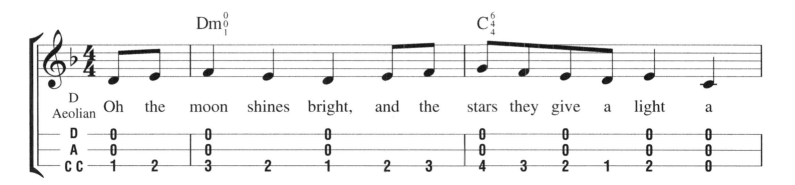

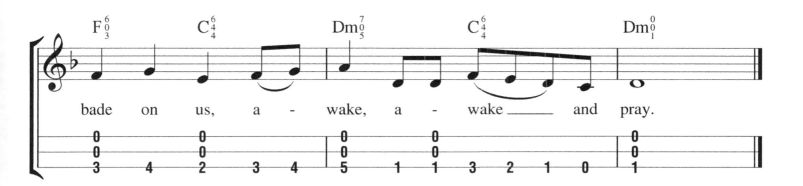

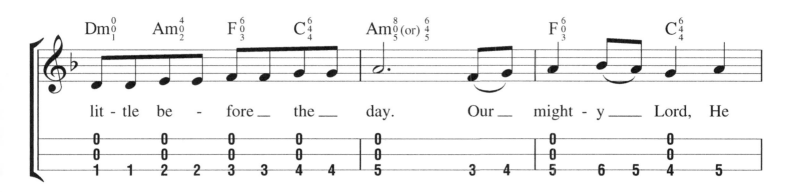

SUGGESTED FINGERING FOR CHORDS:　6(i)
　4(r)
　5(m)

GODDESSES
(Aeolian Version)

Since "Goddesses" does not have a 6th, it can be played in both the Aeolian and Dorian tunings.

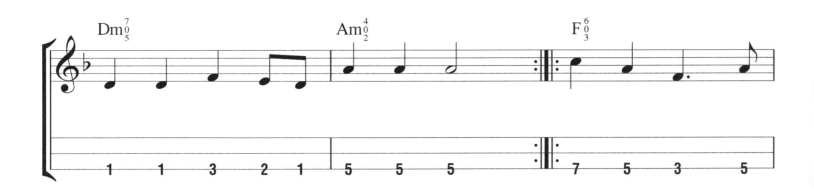

SUGGESTED FINGERING FOR CHORDS:

$$Dm\ {}^{7(i)}_{0}_{5(r)} \quad Am\ {}^{4(i)}_{0}_{2(r)} \quad F\ {}^{6(r)}_{0}_{3(p)} \quad C\ {}^{6(i)}_{4(m)}_{4(r)} \quad Dm\ {}^{0}_{0}_{1(r)} \quad Am\ {}^{4(i)}_{4(m)}_{5(t)}$$

BRETON TUNE

Here is another Aeolian melody to add to your repertoire.

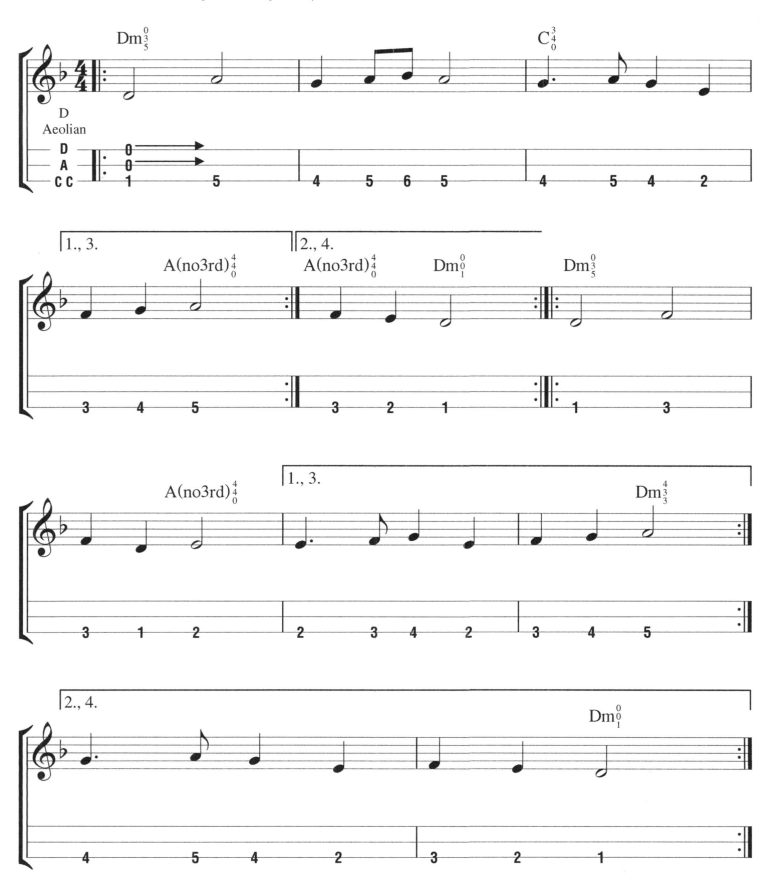

BOLD FENIAN MEN

Notice there is no 6th note in this ballad. Therefore you can also play it in a Dorian tuning. I chose Aeolian because it seems to fit the mood of the ballad.

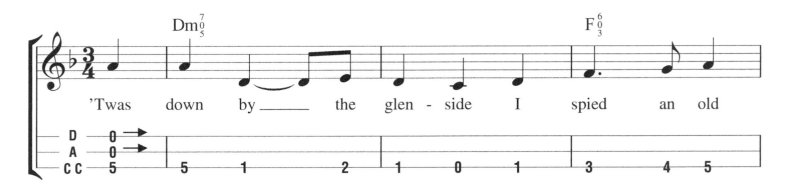

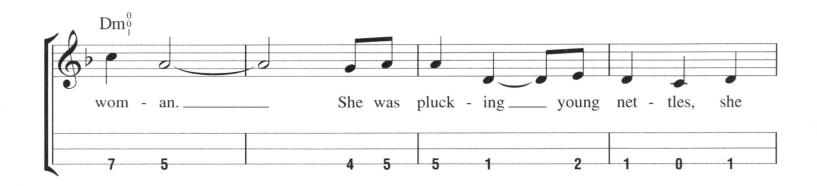

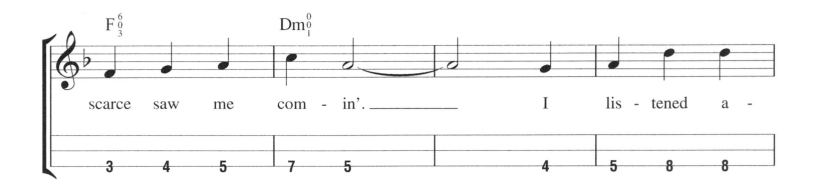

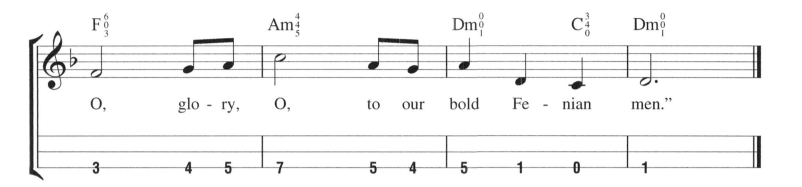

O, glo - ry, O, to our bold Fe - nian men."

        Dm   **F**   **Dm**
2. The sixteen long years since I saw the moon beamin'
                                F   **Dm**
On strong manly forms, and their eyes were heard gleamin'.
                    F   **Am**
I see them all now, sure, in all my day dreamin'.
        F   **Am**   **Dm**   **C Dm**
Glory, O, glory, O, to our bold Fenian men.

        Dm   **F**   **Dm**
3. Some died on the hillside, some died with a stranger.
                             F   **Dm**
And wise men have judged that their cause was a failure.
                         F   **Am**
They fought for their freedom and they never feared danger.
        F   **Am**   **Dm**   **C Dm**
Glory, O, glory, O, to our bold Fenian men.

    Dm   **F**   **Dm**
4. I passed on my way, thanks to God that I met her.
                        F   **Dm**
Be life long or short, I'll never forget her.
                           F   **Am**
There may have been brave men, but there'll never be better.
        F   **Am**   **Dm**   **C Dm**
Glory, O, glory, O, to our bold Fenian men.

THE CUCKOO

Following are several more great tunes in Aeolian and Dorian.

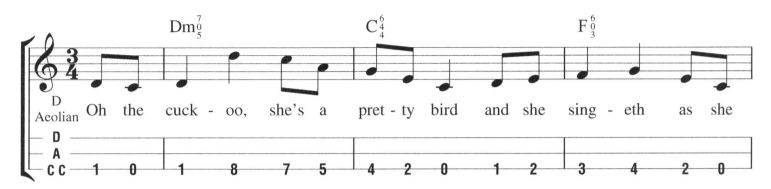

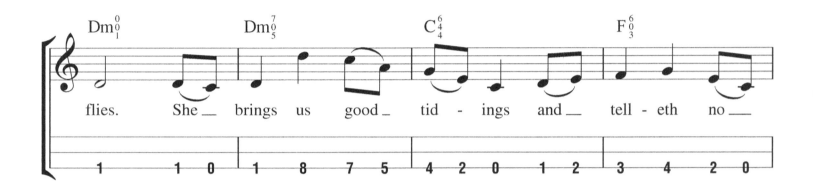

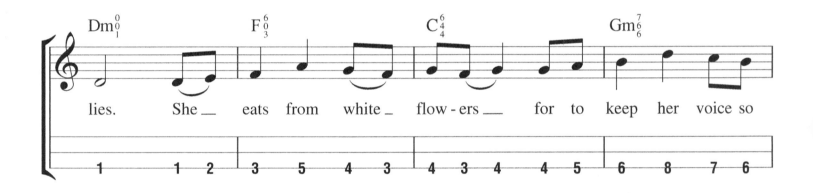

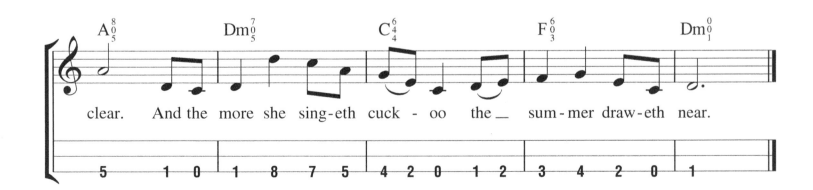

     Dm   **C**   **F**   **Dm**
2. As I was a-walking and a-talking one day,

     Dm   **C**   **F**   **Dm**
I met my own true love as she passed along that way.

         F   **C**   **Gm**   **A**
Oh, the courting was a pleasure, but the parting was woe.

     Dm   **C**   **F**   **Dm**
For I found her false-hearted, she would love me and go.

     Dm   **C**   **F**   **Dm**
3. I wish I was a scholar and could handle the pen.

     Dm   **C**   **F**   **Dm**
I'd write to my own true love and to all you roving men.

        F   **C**   **Gm**   **A**
I would warn them of the grief and woe that attended to their lies.

     Dm   **C**   **F**   **Dm**
I'd wish them to have pity on a flower when it dies.

     Dm   **C**   **F**   **Dm**
4. Come all ye tender maidens and take warning by me,

     Dm   **C**   **F**   **Dm**
And never place affection upon the willow tree.

        F   **C**   **Gm**   **A**
For the leaves they will wither, and the roots they'll soon run dry.

     Dm   **C**   **F**   **Dm**
My own love has forsaken me and I cannot tell you why.

SUGGESTED FINGERING FOR CHORDS:

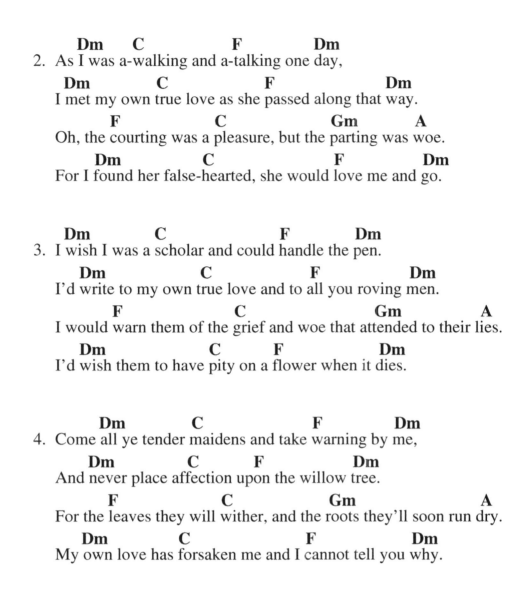

SPAGNOLETTA

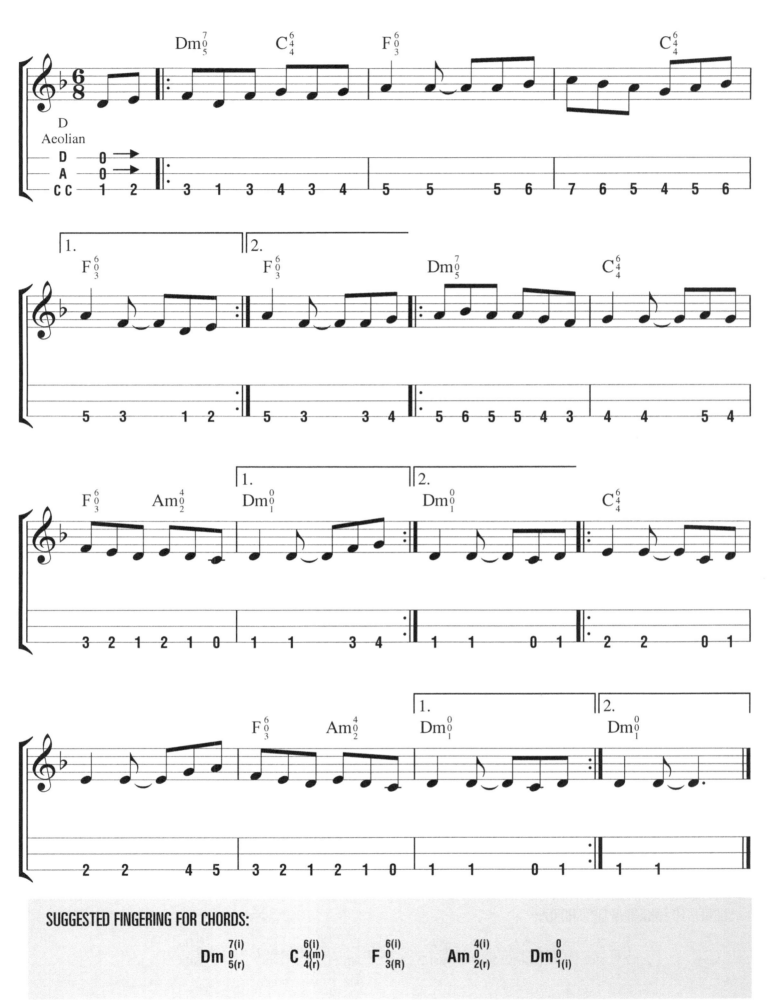

TRALEE JAIL

Please note the new Dorian tuning (DD–A–A). Simply drop the bass string down to an octave lower than the middle string. From DD–A–A, you may tune CC–G–C and play the same fret numbers. However, you will now be playing one whole step lower.

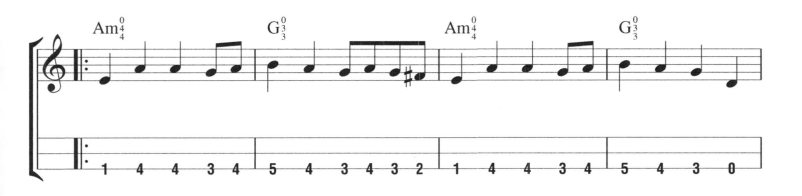

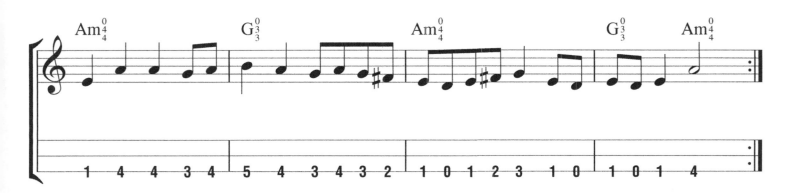

THE WRAGGLE-TAGGLE GYPSIES

A Dorian: There __ were three gyp - sies a - come to my door, and

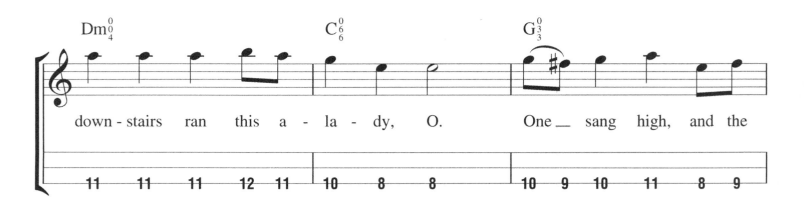

down - stairs ran this a - la - dy, O. One __ sang high, and the

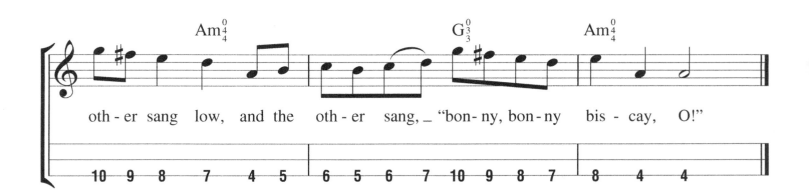

oth - er sang low, and the oth - er sang, __ "bon- ny, bon- ny bis - cay, O!"

Am
2. Then she pulled off her silk-finished gown
    Dm   C
And put on hose of leather-O!
    G   Am
The ragged, ragged rags about our door,
              G   Am
And she's gone with the wraggle, taggle Gypsies, O!

Am
3. It was late last night when my lord came home,
    Dm   C
Inquiring for his a-lady, O!
    G   Am
The servants said on ev'ry hand:
              G   Am
"She's gone with the wraggle-taggle Gypsies, O!"

Am
4. O saddle to me my milk white steed

Dm   **C**
And go fetch me my pony, O!

G   **Am**
That I may ride and seek my bride,

                  G   **Am**
Who is gone with the wraggle-taggle Gypsies, O!

Am
5. O, he rode high and he rode low.

Dm   **C**
He rode through wood and copses too,

G   **Am**
Until he came to a wide open field,

              G   **Am**
And there he espied his a-lady, O!

Am
6. What makes you leave your house and land?

Dm   **C**
What makes you leave your money, O!

G   **Am**
What makes you leave your wedded Lord?

              G   **Am**
To ride with the wraggle-taggle Gypsies, O!

Am
7. What care I for my house and my land?

Dm   **C**
What care I for my money, O!

G   **Am**
What care I for my new wedded Lord?

              G   **Am**
I'm off with the wraggle-taggle Gypsies, O!

Am
8. Last night you slept on a goose feather bed,

Dm   **C**
With the sheet turned down so bravely, O!

G   **Am**
Tonight you'll sleep in a cold, open field,

              G   **Am**
Along with the wraggle-taggle Gypsies, O!

Am
9. What care I for a goose feather bed,

Dm   **C**
With the sheet turned down so bravely, O!

G   **Am**
For tonight I shall sleep in a cold, open field,

              G   **Am**
Along with the wraggle-taggle Gypsies, O!

CLUCK OLD HEN

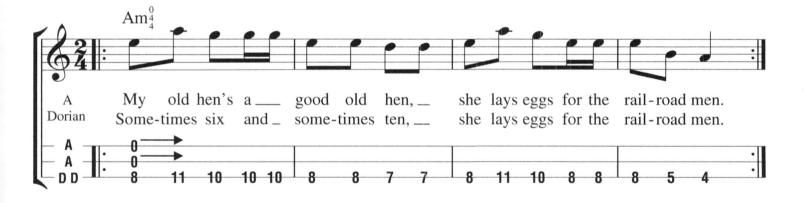

A Dorian

My old hen's a ___ good old hen, ___ she lays eggs for the rail-road men.
Some-times six and ___ some-times ten, ___ she lays eggs for the rail-road men.

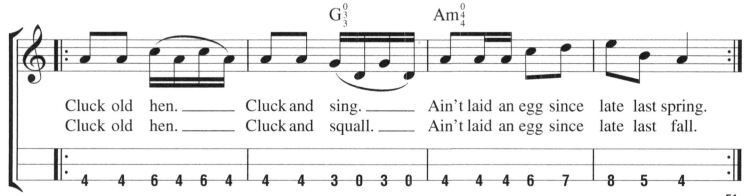

Cluck old hen. _____ Cluck and sing. _____ Ain't laid an egg since late last spring.
Cluck old hen. _____ Cluck and squall. _____ Ain't laid an egg since late last fall.

BRIAN BORU'S MARCH

You may tune to CC–G–D (Gm); the fret numbers will be the same, but the notes will be one step lower.

NOTE: This composition has no 6th. You can therefore play this march in an Aeolian tuning. I chose this tuning because of the key (Am) and the overall sound.

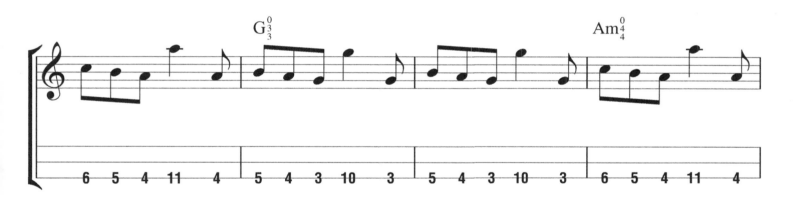

UTILIZING THE EXTRA (6½) FRET

Many dulcimers made today have the extra fret. This fret is placed between the 6th and 7th fret, thus giving it the title of the 6½ fret. To check if you have this fret, first tune your dulcimer to DD–A–D. Now press to the left of the 6th fret melody string. Go to the next fret. If this is a half step (C♯), you have the extra fret. If this is a whole step (D), you don't. (See illustration.)

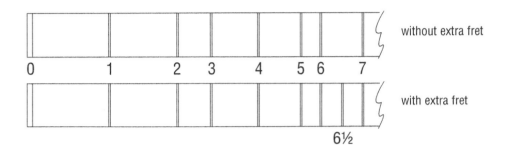

This extra fret is very handy. When used properly it can:

1. Allow you to play a Dorian scale while tuned to an Aeolian mode.

2. Allow you to play an Ionian scale while tuned to the Mixolydian.

Why? With the 6½ fret, the 6th in the Aeolian can be raised a half step so the scale becomes Dorian. The 7th in the Mixolydian can be raised a half step so the scale becomes Ionian.

Aeolian tuning (CC–A–D): By using the 6½ fret, the scale becomes Dorian.

	D	E	F	G	A	B	C	D
Fret #:	1	2	3	4	5	6½	7	8

Mixolydian tuning (DD–A–D): By using the 6½ fret, the scale becomes Ionian.

	D	E	F♯	G	A	B	C♯	D
Fret #:	0	1	2	3	4	5	6½	7

Therefore, your extra 6½ fret allows you to change modes without retuning. The DD–A–D tuning can be used for both Mixolydian and Ionian, and the CC–A–D tuning can be used for Aeolian and Dorian.

THE CHANTER SONG

Let's play the following examples. By using the extra (6½) fret, you are playing in the Dorian mode while tuned to the Aeolian.

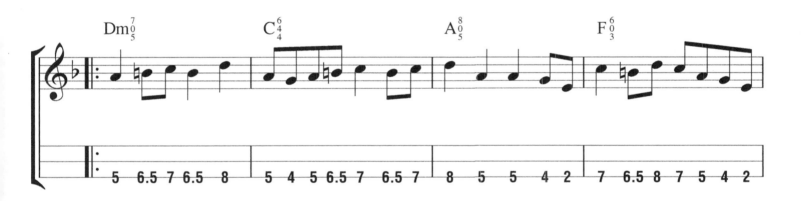

UNCLE JOE

By using the extra fret (6½) in the DD–A–D tuning, you can now play in the Ionian mode.

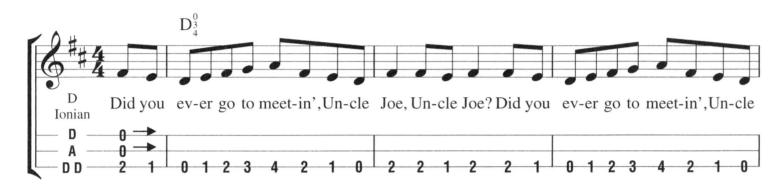

Did you ev-er go to meet-in', Un-cle Joe, Un-cle Joe? Did you ev-er go to meet-in', Un-cle

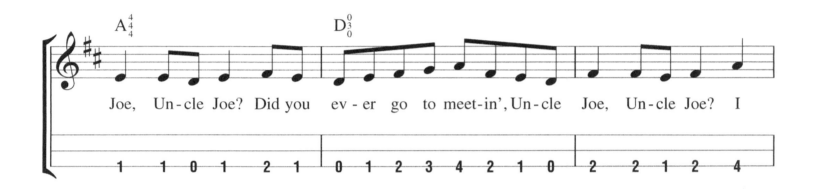

Joe, Un-cle Joe? Did you ev-er go to meet-in', Un-cle Joe, Un-cle Joe? I

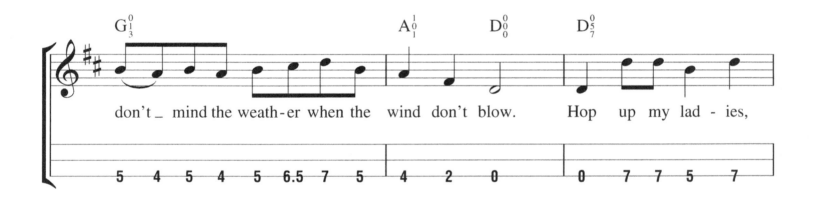

don't _ mind the weath-er when the wind don't blow.   Hop up my lad-ies,

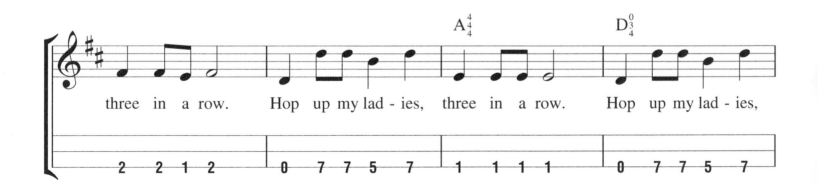

three in a row.   Hop up my lad-ies, three in a row.   Hop up my lad-ies,

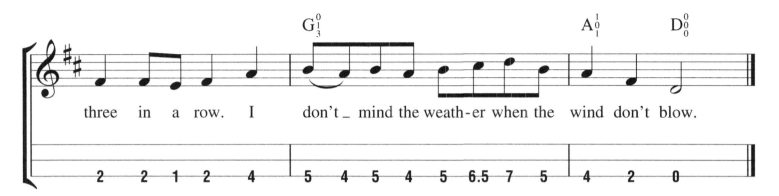

D
1. Did you ever go to meetin', Uncle Joe, Uncle Joe?
                                              A
   Did you ever go to meetin', Uncle Joe, Uncle Joe?
      D
   Did you ever go to meetin', Uncle Joe, Uncle Joe?
    G   A   D
   I don't mind the weather when the wind don't blow.

            D
Chorus Hop up my ladies, three in a row.
                       A
        Hop up my ladies, three in a row.
        D
        Hop up my ladies, three in a row.
         G   A   D
        I don't mind the weather when the wind don't blow.

            D
2. Will your horse carry double, Uncle Joe, Uncle Joe?
   ...
   Chorus

            D
3. Is your horse a single footer, Uncle Joe, Uncle Joe?
   ...
   Chorus

            D
4. Would you rather ride a pacer, Uncle Joe, Uncle Joe?
   ...
   Chorus

            D
5. Have you ever seen the Devil, Uncle Joe, Uncle Joe?
   ...
   Chorus

SUGGESTED FINGERING FOR CHORDS:

$$D \begin{smallmatrix}0\\3(i)\\4(t)\end{smallmatrix} \quad A \begin{smallmatrix}4(i)\\4(m)\\4(r)\end{smallmatrix} \quad D \begin{smallmatrix}0\\3(m)\\0\end{smallmatrix} \quad G \begin{smallmatrix}0\\1(i)\\3(t)\end{smallmatrix} \quad A \begin{smallmatrix}1(i)\\0\\1(m)\end{smallmatrix} \quad D \begin{smallmatrix}0\\5(i)\\7(t)\end{smallmatrix}$$

FINGERPICKING THE DULCIMER

What could be more intimate than fingerpicking a dulcimer? To feel the vibrations of the instrument… to control the rise and fall of the melodic line… that is what fingerpicking is all about!

Where to start? Start with your support system. Use your ring finger and pinky of the right hand to pull the dulcimer into your body by bracing them against the fretboard. With your thumb (t), index (i), and middle (m) fingers, you will be picking or pushing the instrument away from you, so you need this brace to keep the dulcimer from slipping off your lap.

Think of your brace, wrist, and forearm as being one straight unit connected to your elbow. You wrist should be flat, but relaxed.

Now practice picking patterns by using every possible combination of the letters t (thumb), i (index), and m (middle): tim tim, mit mit, timmi timmi, mitti mitti, etc. (By the way, you don't have to have a dulcimer on your lap to practice picking patterns. Your car's steering wheel works just as well. During red lights, brace and pick. You'll be amazed at how fast the light changes and how much your finger dexterity improves!) When you can hold a conversation while picking a pattern, you are ready to add the left hand.

Generally speaking, the melody or tune is played on the highest strings (double strings closest to you). It is easier to hear the high notes over the droning middle and bass strings. Luckily, you will play the melody with your strongest digit: your thumb.

Play the melody picking only with your thumb. Notice which notes last longer. Try to "fill in" the long melody notes by picking with your middle and index fingers. If your note is longer than an eighth ($\eighth$) note, you will have time to pick more notes. By keeping track of the sub-divisions of each beat, you should be able to play in perfect rhythm.

If the melody note has the rhythm ♩ you can play ti;

♩.	=	tim
♩	=	timi
♩.	=	timimi

Sometimes the quarter note is divided into four sixteenth-note pulses. The sixteenth note ($\sixteenth$) is then equal to one pulse.

When dealing with sixteenth-note rhythms, you can use the following picking patterns:

♪.	=	tim
♩	=	timi
♩.	=	timimi

Whenever possible, you should try to vary the pattern to avoid monotony. You can pluck two notes at the same time ($\frac{0}{3}$). This places more stress on important words or beats. You can allow one string to vibrate longer (—) to fill in the missing beats or strum across all three strings at once (⌇).

No matter what picking pattern or style you decide to use, one thing is certain. The melody must be louder than the accompanying notes. Listen to yourself on tape to be sure you can distinguish the difference. Within the melody, some notes may sound louder than others. The primary or strongest accent comes on beat one of every measure. A piece in 4 will feel like "hup 2 3 4." A waltz in 3 should sound "loud soft soft." If your accents are too strong, you will sound mechanical. If they are too weak, you will sound non-rhythmic.

Once you have a good rhythmic flow to your playing, you need to determine the length of the phrase. If standard notation is used, the phrase can be found wherever different notes are under the long curved line. All the notes under the curved line belong together like words in a sentence. When there are no phrase markings, look for punctuation marks in the verse. All the words between commas or periods make a phrase.

Every phrase has one note that's higher and more important than the rest. This note should be the loudest of that phrase—even louder than the primary accents. Every note preceding this high point should build to it in a gradual crescendo. Every note following it should gradually subside until it almost fades away. The higher the note, the louder you should play. The lower the note, the softer you should play. If there are repeated notes, one note will still sound more important than the others, because it is either on a strong beat or an important syllable of a word.

If in doubt, sing the melody. You will sing it correctly—placing stress in points of tension. Make your playing imitate your singing. When you are satisfied with the sound of the melody, add the accompaniment. The accompaniment is still softer than the melody, but now it will reinforce your dynamic plan. Shade the accompaniment into the melody, hinting when you will get louder or softer. Within each phrase, you may have many shades of soft or loud. From phrase to phrase, you may change color or dynamics completely.

Only when you control the sounds are you making music. Otherwise, you are just playing notes. You must feel the song with your fingers and your ears. Then you are breathing life into a melody.

THE BONNIE, BONNIE BANKS OF THE VIRGIO

"The Bonnie, Bonnie Banks of the Virgio" is a haunting melody. The use of the B♭ (lowered 6th) and C♮ (lowered 7th) make this song a perfect example of the Aeolian mode. The tuning is well suited to the ironic conclusion of the story. First learn the song using a strum, then try the fingerpicking.

Notice that the thumb and middle fingers pluck simultaneously when the tab numbers are stacked above each other.

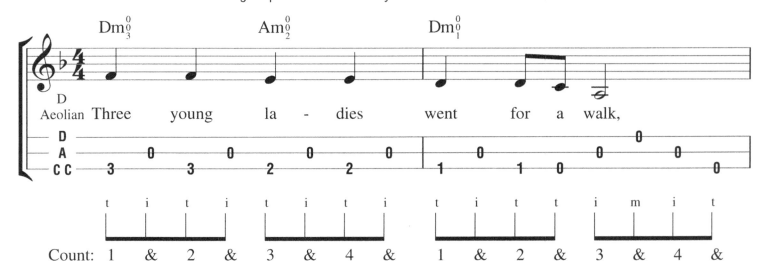

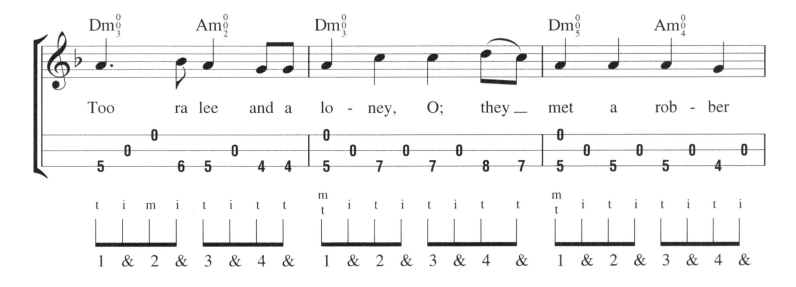

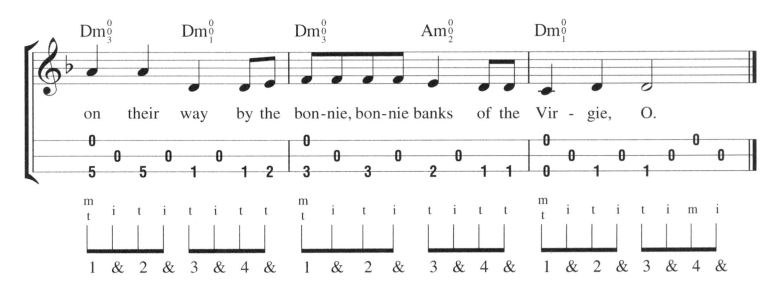

Dm   Am   Dm
1. Three young ladies went for a walk,
          Am   Dm
    Too ra lee and a loney, O;
          Dm Am   Dm
    They met a robber on their way
          Dm   Am   Dm
    By the bonnie, bonnie banks of the Virgie, O.

Dm   Am   Dm
2. He took the first one by the hand,
          Am   Dm
    Too ra lee and a loney, O;
          Dm Am   Dm
    And he whipped her around and he made her stand
          Dm   Am   Dm
    By the bonnie, bonnie banks of the Virgie, O.

3. Will you be a robber's wife, too ra...
    Or will you die by my penknife?
       By the bonnie...

4. I will not be a robber's wife, too ra...
    I'd rather die by my penknife?
       By the bonnie...

5. He took the second one by the hand, too ra...
    And he whipped her around and he made
       Her stand. By the bonnie...

6. Will you be a robber's wife; too ra...
    Or will you die by my penknife?
       By the bonnie...

7. He took the third one by the hand, too ra...
    And he whipped her around and made her stand.
       By the bonnie...

8. Will you be a robber's wife, too ra...
    Or will you die by my penknife?
       By the bonnie...

9. I will not be a robber's wife, too ra...
    Nor will I die by your penknife.
       By the bonnie...

10. If my brothers had been here, too ra...
    You would not have killed my sisters dear.
       By the bonnie...

11. Who are your brothers, I pray you tell?
       Too ra...
    One is a robber like yourself.
       By the bonnie...

12. Who is the other, I pray you tell? Too ra...
    The other is a minister.
       By the bonnie...

13. Lord, have mercy for what I've done;
       Too ra...
    I've killed my sisters, all but one.

LAUDA

A simple pinch pick pattern will do well for this 13th century Italian composition. Use your thumb to pick the melody string(s) and your index for the middle and bass strings. P = pull-off, H = Hammer-on. Please refer to page 66 on three basic embellishments for instruction.

AMAZING GRACE

It is not necessary to pluck a string on each pulsation of a long note. You can also allow the strings to vibrate freely. This helps to provide more variety in an arrangement.

A dash (—) Indicates how many pulsations to wait before continuing with a picking pattern.

2. 'Twas grace that taught my heart to fear,
        D
And grace my fears relieved.
   G   **C**   **G**
How precious did that grace appear,
   D D7 G
The hour I first believed!

3. Through many danger, toils, and snares,
        D
I have already come.
   G   **C**   **G**
His grace has brought me safe thus far,
   D D7 G
His grace will lead me home.

JOHNNY THE SAILOR

"Johnny the Sailor" has a distinctly Dorian sound with its lowered 3rd (F♮) and 7th (C♮) scale tones.

For easier fretting, anchor your middle ring finger of the left hand on fret four of the middle string. Then slide down to fret one and back up again. Use your thumb to slide up and down on the treble string.

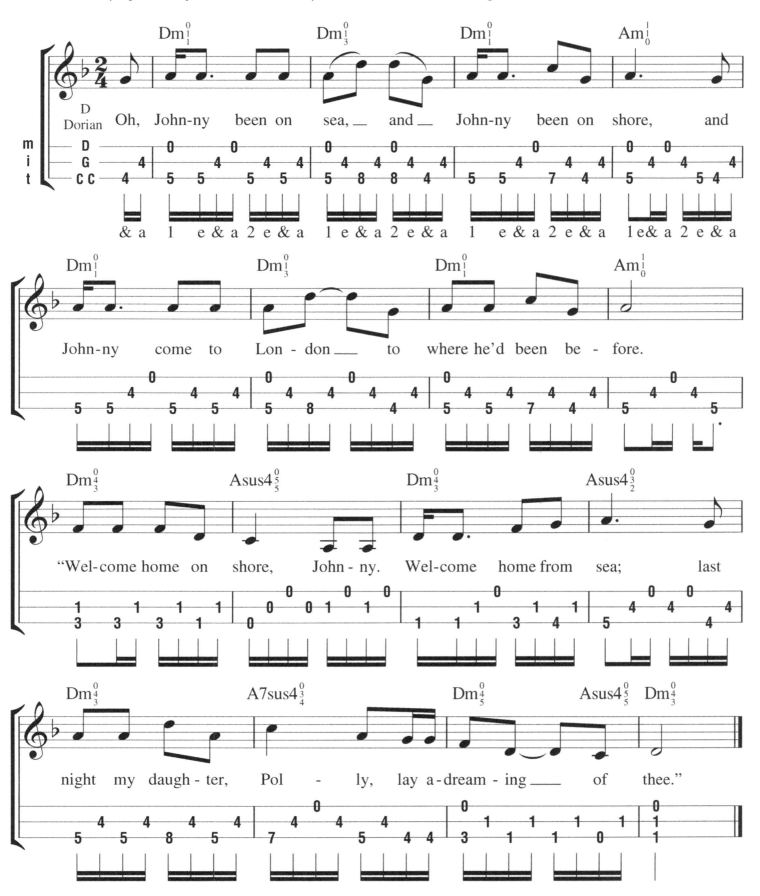

Dm
2. "Go fetch your daughter Polly
                 Am
And set her down by me;
   Dm
By all that's melancholy,
              Am
It's married we will be."
 Dm   **Asus4**
"Oh, what luck, my Johnny boy?"
 Dm   **Asus4**
"Very bad," says he.
     Dm   **A7sus4**
"I've lost my ship and cargo
   Dm   **Asus4 Dm**
All on the raging   sea."

          Dm
3. "My daughter Polly is absent, John,
         Am
And won't return today;
   Dm
But if she was here, John,
           Am
She no would let you stay."
Dm   **Asus4**
Johnny being drowsy
   Dm   **Asus4**
He hanged down his head
  Dm   **A7sus4**
And called for a candle
   Dm   **Asus4 Dm**
To light him up to   bed.

           Dm
4. "My beds are full of strangers,
            Am
Have been all the week,
   Dm
And for another lodging
           Am
You will have to seek."
Dm   **Asus4**
Twenty shillings of the new
 Dm   **Asus4**
And thirty of the old,
   Dm   **A7sus4**
And John pulled out his two
     Dm Asus4 Dm
Hands full of   gold!

          Dm
5. The sight of the money
             Am
Caused the landlady to weep.
   Dm
"My green bed is empty,
           Am
And there you shall sleep."
Dm   **Asus4**
In came daughter Polly
   Dm   **Asus4**
With a smiling face;
   Dm   **A7sus4**
She give him a kiss
     Dm Asus4 Dm
And a fond embrace.

        Dm
6. "Before I had money
           Am
My lodging was to seek;
   Dm
Before I'd sleep in your green bed
          Am
I'd sleep in the street.
Dm   **Asus4**
Now I have got money,
   Dm   **Asus4**
I'll make the taverns whirl,
   Dm   **A7sus4**
With a bottle of good brandy,
   Dm   **Asus4 Dm**
And on each knee a   girl."

THREE BASIC EMBELLISHMENTS

Once you feel comfortable with the preceding arrangements, it might be time to "spruce" them up with some ornamentation. American, English, Irish, Scottish, and European tunes all rely heavily on embellishments. All folk instruments, from the lute to the bagpipe, utilize embellishments to breathe new life, personality, and excitement into the already existing melody. Of course, you can use any tuning, but for now, use DD–A–D.

The Hammer-On: Strum the dulcimer once. With the strings still sounding, bring your index finger down directly to the left of the 1st fret. Pretend your finger is a little hammer and there is a very small nail to the left of this fret you need to hammer in. (See photos.) In most books, the hammer-on is shown by an "H." In our example it would look like this:

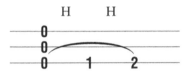

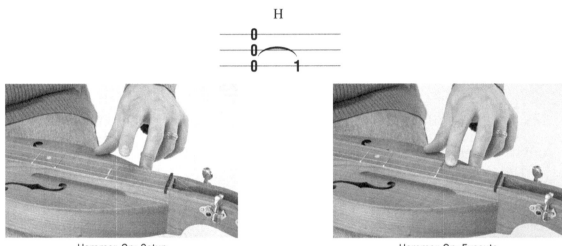

Hammer-On: Setup   Hammer-On: Execute

It's kind of like getting two notes for the price of one. Now let's try a double hammer. Strum the dulcimer open. Hammer your middle finger to the left of the 1st fret and quickly hammer your index finger to the left of the 2nd fret. Presto! Three notes for the price of one. Remember you only strum once; the rest of the notes are sounded with your fretting hand.

Double hammer-on

Double Hammer-On: Setup   Double Hammer-On 1   Double Hammer-On 2

Now try a triple hammer on the first three frets with your ring, middle, and index fingers on frets one, two, and three, respectively. Try this technique starting on the higher frets also.

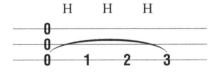

Triple hammer-on

The Pull-Off: Think of this as "kissing" the string goodbye. Put your index finger on the 1st fret. Strum the dulcimer across all of the strings. Now *pull* your finger from the string and at the same time sound the string with your finger as you leave it. This is called a pull-off and is designated by a "P." (See photos.)

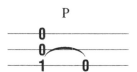

Pull-Off: Setup

Pull-Off: Execute

Now put your middle finger to the left of the 1st fret and your index finger to the left of the 2nd fret. Strum across all your strings. Now pull your index finger from the 2nd fret, pause, and then pull your middle finger from the 1st fret: a double pull.

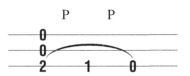

Double pull

Double Pull-Off: Setup

Double Pull-Off 1

Double Pull-Off 2

Now try a triple pull with your ring, middle, and index fingers on the 1st, 2nd, and 3rd frets, respectively:

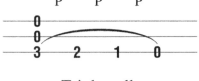

Triple pull

Now let's combine these two embellishments. First a single hammer to a single pull:

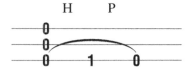

Now a double hammer to a double pull:

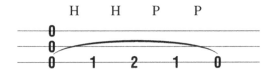

Look out; it's a triple hammer to a triple pull:

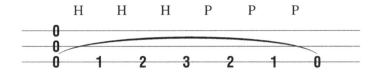

The Slide: Place your middle finger to the left of the 1st fret. Strum across all the strings and slide that finger up to the 2nd fret. A slide is designated by a "sl." Next try double and triple slides.

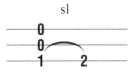

Slide: Setup

Slide: Execute

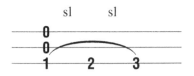

Double slide

Now let's bring it all together with a double hammer to a double slide to a double pull-off:

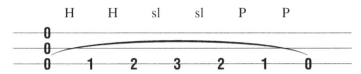

Remember: Use whatever fingers feel right. Some folks like using the thumb, some just fingers. Experiment! Take this knowledge and rearrange the tunes as you like.

JOHN BROSNAN'S POLKA

Check out the following tunes that include many embellishments.

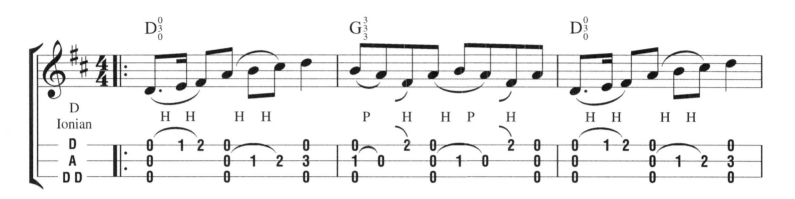

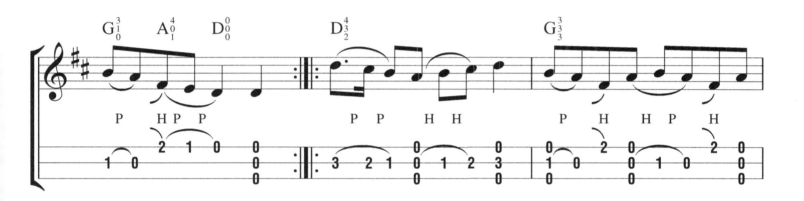

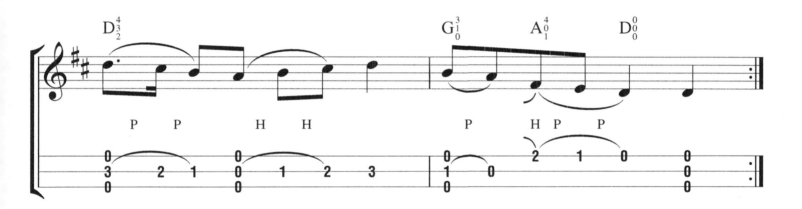

BRETON LULLABYE

By utilizing the 2nd fret of the middle string (C#), one is now playing in an Ionian mode.

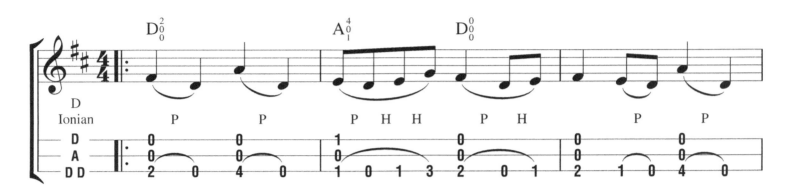

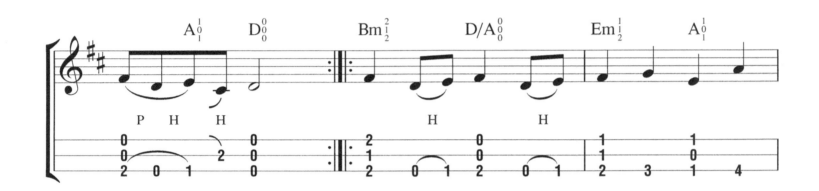

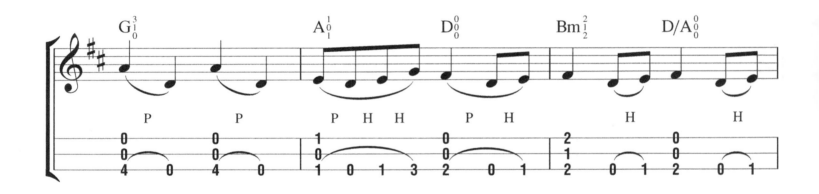

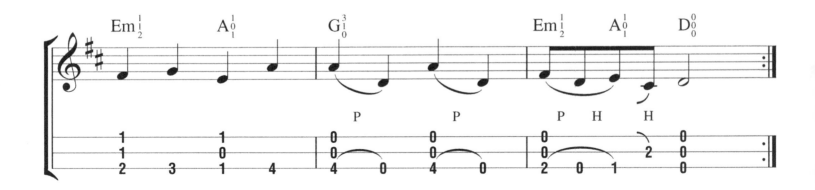

KINGDOM COMING

Play this one slowly at first before you bring it up to speed. This tune is also known as "The Year of Jubilo."

BATTLE CRY OF FREEDOM

SPAGNOLETTA
(Advanced Version)

THE CHANTER SONG
(Advanced Version)

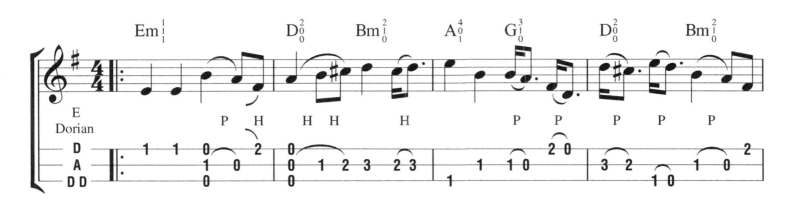

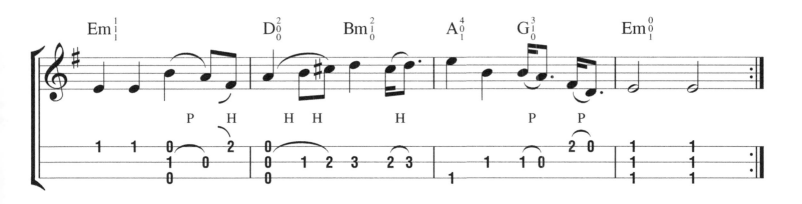

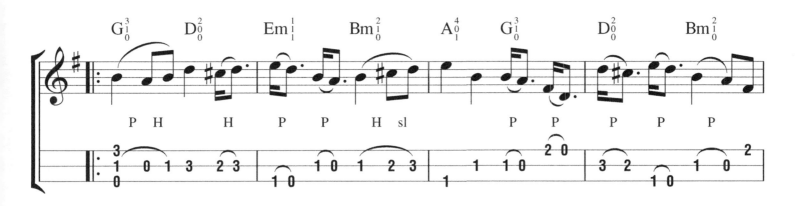

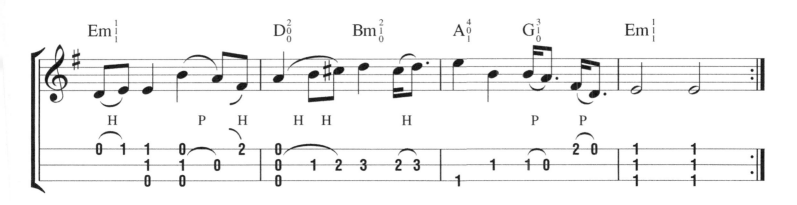

TUNINGS

A Simple Way to Utilize All Six Tunings in This Book

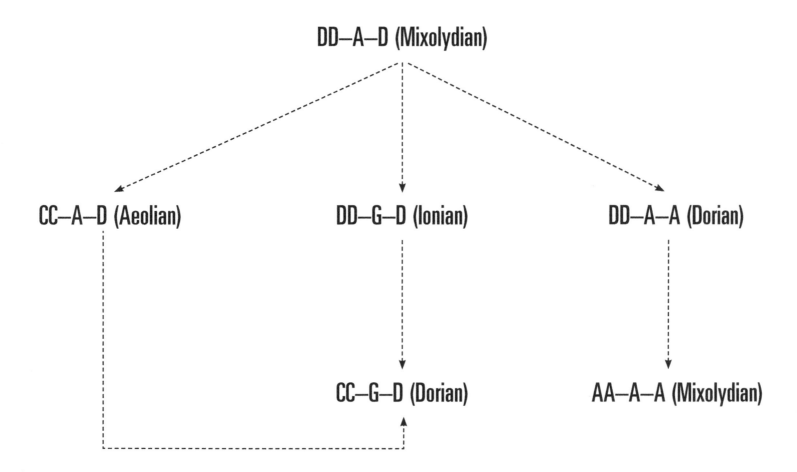

Remember, to use these tunings, please string your dulcimer with the following strings:

Bass: .024 Bronze Wound

Middle: .012-.014

Treble: .010

Be sure to notice if your dulcimer takes ball- or loop-end strings.

MUSICAL SYMBOLS USED IN THIS BOOK

Repeat Signs

Many of the tunes and ballads in this book have repeat signs. These mean that you repeat everything between them once before you go on to the next part.

First and Second Endings

The first ending will always be before the repeat sign. Play the first ending, go back to the repeat sign, play this part again with the second ending. Don't repeat the first ending twice.

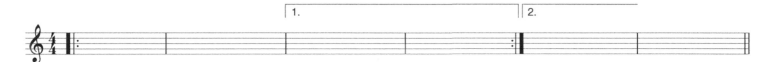

Time Signatures

The number of beats in each measure is written out at the beginning of each song in the time signature. The top number tells you how many beats per measure, and the bottom number tells you the time value of each beat.

3 beats per measure
Quarter note ♩ = one beat

Key Signatures

To tell what key a composition is in, look at the beginning of the staff to see how many sharps (♯) or flats (♭) the song has. A sharp is a half step above the original note, a flat is a half step below.

Ties

When two of more notes of the same pitch are joined by a curved line they are said to be tied and are played as one unbroken sound equal to the sum of the individual notes.

COUNT: 1   2   3 + 4   1   2 + 3   4 +   1   2   3   4 +   1   2 + 3   4

Note Values

Here is a breakdown of the most common note values.

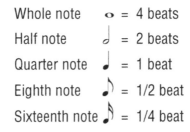

Whole note   = 4 beats
Half note   = 2 beats
Quarter note   = 1 beat
Eighth note   = 1/2 beat
Sixteenth note   = 1/4 beat

Rests

Rests indicate the length of silence between notes. This figure depicts the most common types of rests.

Whole rest	Half rest	Quarter rest	Eighth rest	Sixteenth rest
4 beats	2 beats	1 beat	1/2 beat	1/4 beat

Beams

Two or more sixteenth and eighth notes can be joined together by a beam.

Sixteenth: Eighth:

Dotted Notes

A dot after a note means you hold it 1½ times the value of the original note.

Triplets

A triplet is a group of three notes whose total time value is equal to two notes of the same value.

Quarter note   =   Eighth notes   =   Eighth note triplets

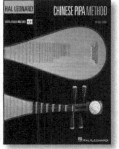

THE ULTIMATE COLLECTION OF
FAKE BOOKS

The Real Book – Sixth Edition

Hal Leonard proudly presents the first legitimate and legal editions of these books ever produced. These bestselling titles are mandatory for anyone who plays jazz! Over 400 songs, including: All By Myself • Dream a Little Dream of Me • God Bless the Child • Like Someone in Love • When I Fall in Love • and more.

00240221   Volume 1, C Instruments...$45.00
00240224   Volume 1, B♭ Instruments...$45.00
00240225   Volume 1, E♭ Instruments...$45.00
00240226   Volume 1, BC Instruments...$45.00

**Go to halleonard.com
to view all *Real Books* available**

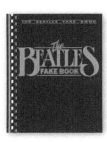

The Beatles Fake Book

200 of the Beatles' hits: All You Need Is Love • Blackbird • Can't Buy Me Love • Day Tripper • Eleanor Rigby • The Fool on the Hill • Hey Jude • In My Life • Let It Be • Michelle • Norwegian Wood (This Bird Has Flown) • Penny Lane • Revolution • She Loves You • Twist and Shout • With a Little Help from My Friends • Yesterday • and many more!
00240069 C Instruments...........$39.99

The Best Fake Book Ever

More than 1,000 songs from all styles of music: All My Loving • At the Hop • Cabaret • Dust in the Wind • Fever • Hello, Dolly • Hey Jude • King of the Road • Longer • Misty • Route 66 • Sentimental Journey • Somebody • Song Sung Blue • Spinning Wheel • Unchained Melody • We Will Rock You • What a Wonderful World • Wooly Bully • Y.M.C.A. • and more.

00290239 C Instruments............................$49.99
00240084 E♭ Instruments............................$49.95

The Celtic Fake Book

Over 400 songs from Ireland, Scotland and Wales: Auld Lang Syne • Barbara Allen • Danny Boy • Finnegan's Wake • The Galway Piper • Irish Rover • Loch Lomond • Molly Malone • My Bonnie Lies Over the Ocean • My Wild Irish Rose • That's an Irish Lullaby • and more. Includes Gaelic lyrics where applicable and a pronunciation guide.
00240153 C Instruments...........$25.00

Classic Rock Fake Book

Over 250 of the best rock songs of all time: American Woman • Beast of Burden • Carry On Wayward Son • Dream On • Free Ride • Hurts So Good • I Shot the Sheriff • Layla • My Generation • Nights in White Satin • Owner of a Lonely Heart • Rhiannon • Roxanne • Summer of '69 • We Will Rock You • You Ain't Seen Nothin' Yet • and lots more!

00240108 C Instruments..............................$35.00

Classical Fake Book

This unprecedented, amazingly comprehensive reference includes over 850 classical themes and melodies for all classical music lovers. Includes everything from Renaissance music to Vivaldi and Mozart to Mendelssohn. Lyrics in the original language are included when appropriate.
00240044 ....$39.99

The Disney Fake Book

Even more Disney favorites, including: The Bare Necessities • Can You Feel the Love Tonight • Circle of Life • How Do You Know? • Let It Go • Part of Your World • Reflection • Some Day My Prince Will Come • When I See an Elephant Fly • You'll Be in My Heart • and many more.
00175311 C Instruments $34.99
Disney characters & artwork TM & © 2021 Disney

The Folksong Fake Book

Over 1,000 folksongs: Bury Me Not on the Lone Prairie • Clementine • The Erie Canal • Go, Tell It on the Mountain • Home on the Range • Kumbaya • Michael Row the Boat Ashore • Shenandoah • Simple Gifts • Swing Low, Sweet Chariot • When Johnny Comes Marching Home • Yankee Doodle • and many more.
00240151 ....$34.99

The Hal Leonard Real Jazz Standards Fake Book

Over 250 standards in easy-to-read authentic hand-written jazz engravings: Ain't Misbehavin' • Blue Skies • Crazy He Calls Me • Desafinado (Off Key) • Fever • How High the Moon • It Don't Mean a Thing (If It Ain't Got That Swing) • Lazy River • Mood Indigo • Old Devil Moon • Route 66 • Satin Doll • Witchcraft • and more.
00240161 C Instruments.................................$45.00

The Hymn Fake Book

Nearly 1,000 multi-denominational hymns perfect for church musicians or hobbyists: Amazing Grace • Christ the Lord Is Risen Today • For the Beauty of the Earth • It Is Well with My Soul • A Mighty Fortress Is Our God • O for a Thousand Tongues to Sing • Praise to the Lord, the Almighty • Take My Life and Let It Be • What a Friend We Have in Jesus • and hundreds more!
00240145 C Instruments..............................$29.99

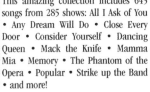

The New Broadway Fake Book

This amazing collection includes 645 songs from 285 shows: All I Ask of You • Any Dream Will Do • Close Every Door • Consider Yourself • Dancing Queen • Mack the Knife • Mamma Mia • Memory • The Phantom of the Opera • Popular • Strike up the Band • and more!
00138905 C Instruments............$45.00

The Praise & Worship Fake Book

Over 400 songs including: Amazing Grace (My Chains Are Gone) • Cornerstone • Everlasting God • Great Are You Lord • In Christ Alone • Mighty to Save • Open the Eyes of My Heart • Shine, Jesus, Shine • This Is Amazing Grace • and more.
00160838 C Instruments $39.99
00240324 B♭ Instruments $34.99

Three Chord Songs Fake Book

200 classic and contemporary 3-chord tunes in melody/lyric/chord format: Ain't No Sunshine • Bang a Gong (Get It On) • Cold, Cold Heart • Don't Worry, Be Happy • Give Me One Reason • I Got You (I Feel Good) • Kiss • Me and Bobby McGee • Rock This Town • Werewolves of London • You Don't Mess Around with Jim • and more.
00240387 ....$34.99

The Ultimate Christmas Fake Book

The 6th edition of this bestseller features over 270 traditional and contemporary Christmas hits: Have Yourself a Merry Little Christmas • I'll Be Home for Christmas O Come, All Ye Faithful (Adeste Fideles) • Santa Baby • Winter Wonderland • and more.
00147215 C Instruments $30.00

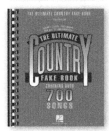

The Ultimate Country Fake Book

This book includes over 700 of your favorite country hits: Always on My Mind • Boot Scootin' Boogie • Crazy • Down at the Twist and Shout • Forever and Ever, Amen • Friends in Low Places • The Gambler • Jambalaya • King of the Road • Sixteen Tons • There's a Tear in My Beer • Your Cheatin' Heart • and hundreds more.
00240049 C Instruments....................................$49.99

The Ultimate Fake Book

Includes over 1,200 hits: Blue Skies • Body and Soul • Endless Love • Isn't It Romantic? • Memory • Mona Lisa • Moon River • Operator • Piano Man • Roxanne • Satin Doll • Shout • Small World • Smile • Speak Softly, Love • Strawberry Fields Forever • Tears in Heaven • Unforgettable • hundreds more!
00240024 C Instruments...........$55.00
00240026 B♭ Instruments......................$49.95

The Ultimate Jazz Fake Book

This must-own collection includes 635 songs spanning all jazz styles from more than 9 decades. Songs include: Maple Leaf Rag • Basin Street Blues • A Night in Tunisia • Lullaby of Birdland • The Girl from Ipanema • Bag's Groove • I Can't Get Started • All the Things You Are • and many more!
00240079 C Instruments................$45.00
00240080 B♭ Instruments....................$45.00
00240081 E♭ Instruments....................$45.00

The Ultimate Rock Pop Fake Book

This amazing collection features nearly 550 rock and pop hits: American Pie • Bohemian Rhapsody • Born to Be Wild • Clocks • Dancing with Myself • Eye of the Tiger • Proud Mary • Rocket Man • Should I Stay or Should I Go • Total Eclipse of the Heart • Unchained Melody • When Doves Cry • Y.M.C.A. • You Raise Me Up • and more.
00240310 C Instruments..................................$39.99

**Complete songlists available online at
www.HalLeonard.com**